THE PATRON

APOLLO
ENCYCLOPEDIA

ᚣᛋᛏᛒᛞᛇᚢᛁᛑᚪᚱᚳᚷᛈ
ᚻᛏᛁᛋᛋᛗᚪᚱᛞᛉᛟᚢᛠ
ᛁᛑᚪᚱᚳᚷᛋᛏᛒᛗᚪᛇ
ᛞᛉᛟᛡᛖᚦᚻᛏᛁᛋᛋᚷᛋᛏ
ᚣᛋᛏᛒᛋᛖᚢᛁᛑᚪᚱᚳᚷᛈᚻ
ᛈᚢᛏᛁᛋᚠᛗᚪᚱᛉᛇᛞᚢ
ᚢᛑᚪᚱᚳᛋᚷᛋᛏᛒᛗᚪᛁ
ᚪᚱᛇᛞᛟᛠᛈᚻᛏᛁᛋᛋᚷᚣ

THE PATRON Apollo MASTER
—ENCYCLOPEDIA—

INTERNATIONAL SALE OF GOODS

CARRIAGE OF GOODS BY SEA

MARTIN APOLLO — AUTHOR
MARWAN M. ALARJAN — AUTHOR
MARTIN APOLLO BUREAU — CONTRIBUTOR

THE PATRON
Master Degree Encyclopedia

The International Trade Law

— INTERNATIONAL SALE OF GOODS —

— CARRIAGE OF GOODS BY SEA —

Martin Apollo Bureau
Research Encyclopedia

By

Martin Apollo
Marwan M. Alarjan

CONTRIBUTOR BY

Martin Apollo Bureau

PART TWO
Of Eight Parts Of Apollo Encyclopedia

INTERNATIONAL SALE OF GOODS
&
CARRIAGE OF GOODS BY SEA

AUTHORS

Marwan M. Alarjan

Martin Apollo

CO-WRITERS

Christopher Attard

Kenneth S. Calleja

Elijah Micallef

Charlene Muscat

Andrew J. Gauci

Fiona Mayor

Dean Cesar

EDITOR

Ghada M. Alarjan

THE ROADMAP

••••••••••••••

••••••••••••••

CHAPTER I
INTERNATIONAL SALE OF GOODS

- INTRODUCTION
- Definition of Importance
- Key Principles and Concepts

TOPIC 1: THE UNITED NATIONS CONVENTION ON CONTRACTS FOR THE INTERNATIONAL SALE OF GOODS (CISG)

- Overview and Historical Context
- Scope and Application
- Key Provisions and Principles
- Case Law and Interpretation
- Role of Case Law in Clarifying Provisions
- Uniform Application and Legal Certainty
- Practical Issues and Business Guidance
- Handling Non-Conforming Goods
- Interpretation Across Jurisdictions
- Impact on Global Trade
- Challenges and Harmonization
- Role of Scholarly Commentary
- Conclusion

TOPIC 2: THE 1980 UNITED NATIONS CONVENTION ON CONTRACTS FOR THE INTERNATIONAL SALE OF GOODS (CISG) AND THE COMMON LAW. IS THERE A PROBLEM?

- Contract Formation
- The Parol Evidence Rule
- Fundamental Breach
- Contract Interpretation
- Remedies for Breach
- Good Faith
- Role of Precedent
- Practical Implications For Businesses
- Harmonization Efforts

Conclusion

TOPIC 3: CHALLENGES AND CRITICISMS

TOPIC 4: HARMONIZATION EFFORTS AND FUTURE PROSPECTS

TOPIC 5: KEY CONTRACTS IN INTERNATIONAL SALES

- FOB (Free on Board) Contract
- CIF (Cost, Insurance, and Freight) Contract
- C&F (Cost and Freight) Contract
- FAS (Free Alongside Ship) Contract

TOPIC 6: DEFINITIONS AND OBLIGATIONS UNDER EACH CONTRACT

- FOB (Free on Board) Contract
- CIF (Cost, Insurance, and Freight) Contract
- C&F (Cost and Freight) Contract
- FAS (Free Alongside Ship) Contract
- Comparison and Implications
- Risk Management
- Dispute Resolution
- Legal Considerations

Conclusion

TOPIC 7: CASE STUDIES AND PRACTICAL CONSIDERATIONS

Case Studies:
- Case Study 1: FOB Contract in Electronics Shipment
- Case Study 2: CIF Contract for Agricultural Products
- Case Study 3: C&F Contract for Industrial Machinery
- Case Study 4: FAS Contract for Bulk Commodities

Practical Considerations:
- Nature of Goods
- Logistics Capabilities
- Cost and Risk Management
- Legal Regulatory Environment

Conclusion

TOPIC 8: THE FAVOR OF CHOOSING CIF CONTRACT RATHER THAN FOB CONTACT

Advantages of CIF Contracts:
- Inclusion of Insurance : A Safety Net
- Simplified Logistics For Buyers
- Cost predictability and financial planning
- Reducing risk exposure for buyers
- Enhanced trust and reliability
- Compliance with international trade norms
- Flexibility and negotiation leverage
- Streamlined dispute resolution
- Market expansion opportunities
- Prompting long-term business relationships

Comparative analysis with FOB contracts:
- Introduction to FOB and CIF contracts
- Risk allocation
- Transportation responsibilities
- Insurance coverage
- Cost implications
- Flexibility and control

- Suitability for different types of Goods
- Legal and Jurisdictional considerations
- Case Study : Electronics shipment under FOB contract
- Case Study: Perishable Goods Shipment under CIF Contract
- Practical Considerations for Businesses
- Negotiation Dynamics
- Impact on Trade Relationships
- Risk Management Strategies
- Compliance with International Standards
- Training and Education for Practitioners
- Technological Advancements and Contract Management
- Future Trends and Developments
- Conclusion: Strategic Decision-Making
- Final Thoughts

Legal and Practical Considerations:
- Introduction
- Nature of the Goods
- Logistical Capabilities
- Specific Transaction Requirements
- Legal Implications: Allocation of Risk

- Cost Responsibilities
- Compliance with International Laws
- Minimizing Dispute Risks
- Case Study: Perishable Goods in CIF Contracts
- Case Study: Electronics Shipment in FOB Contracts
- Role of Insurance in CIF Contracts
- Control Over Logistics in FOB Contracts
- Practical Considerations for Drafting Contracts
- Impact on Trade Relationships
- Negotiation Dynamics
- Legal Framework and Compliance
- Training and Professional Development
- Technological Advancements
- Future Trends and Developments
- Conclusion

Case Studies and Industry Preferences:
- Introduction
- The Shipping Industry and CIF Contracts
- Bulk Commodities: Risk Management and Logistics

- Case Study: Oil Transportation
- The Electronics Industry and FOB Contracts
- High-Value Goods: Control and Customization
- Case Study: Semiconductor Shipment
- The Fashion Industry: A Mixed Approach
- High-End Fashion: Ensuring Safe Transit
- Bulk Fashion Shipments: Cost-Effective Logistics
- Case Study: Luxury Handbags
- Case Study: Mass-Market Apparel
- The Automotive Industry: Managing Complexity
- High-Value Components: Risk Mitigation
- Case Study: Engine Importation
- The Pharmaceutical Industry: Ensuring Integrity
- Sensitive Products: Controlled Environments
- Case Study: Vaccine Distribution
- Industry Preferences and Contract Selection
- Conclusion

TOPIC 9: Comparison with Other Legal Systems

Civil Law vs. Common Law Approaches:
- Introduction to Civil Law and Common Law Systems
- Historical Context and Evolution
- Structure and Sources of Law
- Contract Formation in Civil Law
- Contract Formation in Common Law
- Interpretation of Contracts in Civil Law
- Interpretation of Contracts in Common Law
- The Parol Evidence Rule
- Remedies for Breach of Contract in Civil Law
- Remedies for Breach of Contract in Common Law
- Case Study: Application of Civil Law in International Sales
- Case Study: Application of Common Law in International Sales
- Impact on International Arbitration
- The Role of UNCITRAL and the CISG

- Practical Considerations for Businesses
- Harmonization Efforts and Challenges
- Future Prospects for Harmonization
- Comparative Advantages and Disadvantages
- Conclusion
- Final Thoughts

Impact on International Trade Practices :
- Introduction to Legal Influences on Trade Practices
- Contract Drafting: Emphasis on Formal Requirements vs. Flexibility
- Negotiation Strategies: Structured Processes vs. Adaptive Approaches
- Enforcement Mechanisms: Predictability vs. Judicial Discretion
- Dispute Resolution: Formal Adjudication vs. Alternative Mechanisms
- Risk Allocation: Codified Rules vs. Contractual Flexibility
- Case Study: Civil Law Influence on Contract Management
- Case Study: Common Law Influence on Contract Management

- Legal Certainty and Business Confidence
- Impact on Trade Logistics
- Case Study: Logistics in Civil Law Jurisdictions
- Case Study: Logistics in Common Law Jurisdictions
- Cross-Border Legal Compliance
- Impact on Contractual Remedies
- Case Study: Remedies in Civil Law Jurisdictions
- Case Study: Remedies in Common Law Jurisdictions
- Influence on Business Strategies
- Legal Training and Expertise
- The Role of International Organizations
- Conclusion: Harmonizing Legal Systems for Global Trade

TOPIC 10: Issues and Challenges in the International Sale of Goods

Risk Allocation and Liability:
- Importance of Risk Allocation in International Sales
- Role of Contract Types in Risk Allocation
- FOB Contracts and Risk Allocation
- CIF Contracts and Risk Allocation
- C&F Contracts and Risk Allocation
- Legal Frameworks and Risk Allocation
- Practical Considerations in Risk Allocation
- Case Study: FOB Contract in Practice
- Case Study: CIF Contract in Practice
- Case Study: C&F Contract in Practice
- Drafting Contracts to Address Risk Allocation
- The Role of Insurance in Risk Management
- Addressing Potential Disputes
- The Impact of Transportation Methods
- Regulatory Compliance and Risk Management

- The Role of Technology in Risk Management
- The Interplay of Legal Systems
- The Importance of Clear Communication
- Mitigating Risks Through Contingency Planning

Conclusion: Effective Risk Management in International Sales

TOPIC 11: Dispute Resolution Mechanisms

Importance of Dispute Resolution Mechanisms:
- Arbitration as a Preferred Mechanism
- Benefits and Drawbacks of Arbitration
- Mediation: A Collaborative Approach
- The Role of Litigation in International Disputes
- Enforcement of Arbitration Awards
- Enforcement of Court Judgments
- Case Study: Arbitration in Practice
- Case Study: Mediation in Practice
- Drafting Effective Dispute Resolution Clauses
- Choosing the Appropriate Dispute Resolution Mechanism
- The Role of Legal Advisors
- International Institutions and Dispute Resolution
- Impact of Technological Advances
- Challenges and Criticisms of Arbitration

- Challenges and Criticisms of Mediation
- Future Trends in Dispute Resolution
Conclusion: The Evolving Landscape of Dispute Resolution

TOPIC 12: Impact of Digitalization and E-Commerce

- Impact of Digitalization and E-Commerce
- Data Protection and Privacy Concerns
- Adapting Traditional Legal Principles
- Leveraging Opportunities in the Digital Economy
- Future Trends and Emerging Issues

....

....

CHAPTER II
CARRIAGE OF GOODS BY SEA

- Overview of Maritime Law
- Historical Evolution and Sources of Maritime Law
- Key Principles of Maritime Law
- Carriage of Goods and Marine Insurance
- Ship Ownership and Registration
- Maritime Liens and Claims
- Rights and Responsibilities of Shipmasters, Crew, and Passengers
- Challenges and Future Directions in Maritime Law

Conclusion

TOPIC 1: International Conventions

- Role and Importance of International Conventions

The Hague-Visby Rules: Overview and Impact

- Criticisms of the Hague-Visby Rules:
- The Hamburg Rules: A More Shipper-Friendly Approach

The Rotterdam Rules: Modernizing Maritime Law

- Challenges in Implementing the Rotterdam Rules
- Harmonization vs. Regional Specificities
- The Role of International Bodies in Promoting Conventions

Case Studies: Impact of International Conventions

- Future Directions and Prospects

Hague-Visby Rules :

- Key Provisions and Scope
- Key Provisions and Scope
- Liability Limits and Defenses

- Impact on International Trade
- Criticisms and Limitations
- Comparison with Other Conventions
- Case Law and Interpretation
- Practical Challenges
- Relevance in Modern Shipping
- Future Prospects

Hamburg Rules :
- Introduction and Historical Context
- Extended Carrier Liability Period
- Simplified Claims Procedure
- Increased Carrier Responsibilities
- Liability for Delay
- Wider Applicability
- Limited Adoption
- Industry Resistance
- Comparative Analysis with the Rotterdam Rules
- Future Prospects and Recommendations

Rotterdam Rules:
- Introduction to the Rotterdam Rules
- Comprehensive Coverage of Transport Contracts

- Provisions for Electronic Commerce
- Enhanced Shipper and Carrier Responsibilities
- Extended Liability Periods
- Limited Adoption and Ratification
- Industry Resistance and Concerns
- Comparative Analysis with Previous Conventions
- Potential for Future Adoption
- Conclusion and Future Prospects

TOPIC 2: Bills of Lading and Their Legal Implications

- Introduction to Bills of Lading
- Historical Context and Evolution
- Function as a Receipt
- Evidence of the Contract of Carriage
- Document of Title
- Legal Implications for Carriers

- Legal Implications for Shippers
- Electronic Bills of Lading (eBLs)

Functions of a Bill of Lading:
- Receipt of Goods
- Evidence of Contract
- Document of Title
- Practical Scenario Example

Types of Bills of Lading:
- Straight Bill of Lading
- Order Bill of Lading
- Bearer Bill of Lading
- Practical Scenario Example
- conclusion

Legal Implications:
- Liabilities
- Rights of Holders
- Transferability

TOPIC 3: Liability of Carriers and Shippers

Carrier's Liability:
- Period of Responsibility
- Limits of Liability
- Exceptions to Liability

Shipper's Liability:
- Proper Declaration
- Packaging and Labeling
- Compliance with Regulations

TOPIC 4: Recent Developments and Case Studies

- Electronic Documentation
- Cybersecurity
- Autonomous Shipping

Case Study : Electronic Bills of Lading:
-   Environmental Regulations
- MARPOL Annex VI

- Ballast Water Management Convention

Case study : Implementation of Low-Sulfur Fuel Regulations:

- Trade Practices and Economic Shifts
- Trade Wars and Tariffs
- COVID-19 Pandemic

Case Study: Impact of COVID-19 on Maritime Contracts:

- Regulatory Changes and International Cooperation
- Polar Code
- EU Regulations

Case Study: Compliance with the Polar Code:

- Legal Precedents and Case Law
- Liability and Compensation
- Dispute Resolution

Case Study: Arbitration in Charter Party Disputes:

- Future Trends and Prospects
- Digitalization
- Global Cooperation
- Conclusion

Main Case Study: The Ever Given Incident

Background and Context

Carrier Liability:

- Legal Framework

- Jurisprudence and Precedents

General Average:

- Application in the Ever Given Case

- Legal Analysis

Insurance Claims:

- Types of Insurance Involved:

  - Hull and Machinery Insurance

  - Cargo Insurance

  - Protection and Indemnity (P&I) Insurance

- Jurisprudence and Insurance Law

Operational and Logistical Challenges:

- Supply Chain Disruptions

- Port Congestion

Legal and Financial Implications:

- Claims and Compensation

- Regulatory Reforms

Technological and Environmental Considerations:
- **Technological Improvements**
- **Environmental Impact**

Conclusion

Main Case Study: The MSC Zoe

Background and Context:

Carrier's Liability:

- Legal Framework
- Case Law and Precedents
- Responsibility and Negligence

Environmental Impact:

- Extent of Damage
- Legal Responsibility
- Regulatory Response

Technological Solutions:

- Role of Technology
- Innovation and Implementation
- Case Law and Technological Adoption

Legal and Financial Implications:

- Claims and Compensation
- General Average and Contributions

Operational and Logistical Challenges:

- Supply Chain Disruptions
- Port Congestion

Regulatory and Policy Considerations:
- **Policy Reforms**
- **International Collaboration**

Technological and Environmental Considerations:
- **Environmental Technologies**
- **Sustainability Initiatives**

Conclusion

TOPIC 5: Challenges and Criticisms

Regulatory Fragmentation:
- Introduction to Regulatory Fragmentation
- Impact on Dispute Resolution
- Challenges in Enforcement
- The Role of International Conventions
- Hague-Visby Rules vs. Hamburg Rules
- Rotterdam Rules: A Unified Solution?
- Economic Implications of Fragmentation
- Operational Challenges
- Environmental and Safety Regulations
- Case Study: The MSC Zoe Incident
- Legal Certainty and Predictability
- Harmonization Efforts
- Technological Advancements and Fragmentation
- Impact on Developing Nations
- Role of Regional Agreements
- Insurance and Liability Issues
- Future Directions
- Stakeholder Collaboration

TOPIC 6: Complexity and Costs

Introduction to Complexity and Costs in Maritime Law:
- Multiple Jurisdictions and Legal Frameworks
- Extensive Documentation Requirements
- Legal Principles and International Conventions
- Impact on Small and Medium-sized Enterprises (SMEs)
- Administrative Burden and Operational Efficiency
- Costs of Dispute Resolution
- Insurance and Liability Considerations
- Technological Advances and Regulatory Adaptation
- Environmental Regulations and Compliance Costs

- Case Study: Compliance Costs in the Shipping Industry
- Harmonization of International Regulations
- The Role of Legal Expertise
- Impact on Freight Rates and Shipping Costs
- Strategic Approaches to Managing Costs
- Training and Education
- Collaboration and Industry Best Practices
- Future Trends and Developments
- Policy Recommendations
- Conclusion

TOPIC 7: Environmental Concerns

Introduction to Environmental Concerns in Maritime Law:
- Greenhouse Gas Emissions and Climate Change
- Marine Pollution and the MARPOL Convention
- Ballast Water Management
- Air Pollution and Sulphur Emissions
- Environmental Compliance Costs
- Technological Innovations for Environmental Sustainability
- Economic Impacts of Environmental Regulations
- Port State Control and Environmental Enforcement
- Corporate Social Responsibility and Sustainable Shipping
- Case Study: The Impact of the IMO 2020 Sulphur Cap
- Legal and Regulatory Challenges
- Role of International Collaboration

- Future Directions in Maritime Environmental Law
- Practical Strategies for Compliance
- Conclusion: Balancing Environmental and Commercial Interests
- Case Study: The Implementation of the Polar Code
- Innovative Solutions and Best Practices
- Role of Non-Governmental Organizations (NGOs) and Advocacy
- Conclusion: A Sustainable Path Forward

TOPIC 8: potential reforms and evolving trends

Harmonization of Regulations:
- Importance of Harmonization
- Challenges in Harmonization
- Role of International Conventions

- Economic Implications
- Environmental Considerations
- Technological Advancements
- Impact on Smaller Jurisdictions
- Navigating Political Dynamics
- Future Directions
- Conclusion

TOPIC 9: Digitalization and Technology

Revolutionizing Documentation Processes:
- Enhancing Transparency and Traceability
- Improving Security and Reducing Risks
- Streamlining Customs and Regulatory Compliance
- Boosting Operational Efficiency
- Facilitating Data-Driven Decision Making
- Challenges in Implementation
- Adapting to Technological Change
- Regulatory and Policy Considerations
- Future Prospects and Conclusion

TOPIC 10: Sustainability and Green Shipping

Environmental Imperatives and Regulatory Pressure:
- Advancements in Green Shipping Technologies
- Economic and Operational Challenges
- Impact on Global Supply Chains
- The Role of Digitalization and Data Analytics
- Collaborative Efforts and Industry Initiatives
- Consumer and Market Pressures
- Future Prospects and Innovations
- Challenges and Solutions
- Conclusion

TOPIC 11: Enhanced Liability Frameworks

Modernizing Liability Limits:
- Balancing Interests of Carriers and Shippers
- Addressing Emerging Risks
- Improving Transparency and Accountability
- Adopting a Collaborative Approach
- Incorporating Technological Advancements
- Economic Implications
- Legal Harmonization
- Enhancing Dispute Resolution Mechanisms
- Ensuring Future-Proof Frameworks

TOPIC 12: Improved Dispute Resolution Mechanisms

The Importance of Efficient Dispute Resolution:
- Arbitration as a Preferred Method
- Mediation: A Collaborative Approach

- The Role of Specialized Maritime Courts
- Challenges in Implementing Specialized Courts
- Improving Accessibility and Efficiency
- Balancing Formal and Informal Methods
- Enhancing International Cooperation
- Addressing Cultural Differences
- Adapting to Technological Advances
- Ensuring Fairness and Impartiality
- Managing Costs and Resources
- Promoting Early Resolution
- Integrating Environmental Considerations
- Developing Standardized Procedures
- Enhancing Training and Education
- Utilizing Data and Analytics
- Incorporating Feedback and Continuous Improvement
- Ensuring Global Relevance
- Future Prospects and Innovations

TOPIC 13: Comprehensive Analysis: Practical Scenarios in Carriage of Goods by Sea

- Scenario: Goods Damaged During Transit
- Scenario: Late Delivery and Penalties
- Scenario: Mis-delivery of Goods
- Scenario: Dispute Over Freight Charges
- Scenario: Piracy and Risk Allocation
- Scenario: Environmental Compliance and Fines
- Scenario: Customs Delays and Perishable Goods
- Scenario: Shortage of Delivered Goods
- Scenario: Contract Termination and Goods in Transit
- Scenario: Technological Disruptions

TOPIC 14: Advanced Logic Recommendations for Carriage by Sea

- Risk Assessment and Management
- Optimization of Contract Terms
- Leveraging Technology
- Enhancing Legal and Regulatory Compliance
- Strengthening Dispute Resolution Mechanisms
- Sustainable and Green Shipping Practices
- Collaboration and Partnerships

TOPIC 15: Upcoming Question

Overview of the M/V Ever Given Incident
Legal and Financial Implications:
- Carrier Liability
- General Average
- Insurance Claims

Case Complexity:
- Multi-jurisdictional Issues
- Salvage Operations
- Impact on Global Supply Chains

Case Outcomes and Precedents:
- Settlement and Compensation
- Regulatory and Policy Changes
- Future Legal Implications

Advanced Question for Analysis
Conclusion

Upcoming Parts ...

Encyclopedia — **- THE PATRON -** — .47

THE PATRON

APOLLO
Encyclopedia

Marwan M. Alarjan — **- MASTR -** — Martin Apollo Bureau

CHAPTER ONE
INTERNATIONAL SALE OF GOODS

— Introduction —

Definition and Importance ..

The sale of goods is a cornerstone of international commerce, involving transactions where tangible, movable items are exchanged for monetary value. These transactions are pivotal for global trade, fostering economic integration and development. They enable the efficient allocation of resources across borders, contributing to economic growth and consumer welfare. The sale of goods encompasses various principles and concepts that ensure these transactions are conducted smoothly and equitably, including contract formation, transfer of risk and property, and the obligations of buyers and sellers. The legal frameworks governing the sale of goods, such as the United Nations Convention on Contracts for the International Sale of Goods (CISG), provide standardized rules that facilitate these transactions on a global scale.

The importance of the sale of goods in the global economy cannot be overstated. It facilitates the exchange of products and services across different jurisdictions, allowing countries to specialize in producing goods where they have a comparative advantage. This specialization leads to more efficient production and a higher standard of living worldwide. For example, a country with abundant natural resources but limited technological capabilities can export raw materials to a technologically advanced country, which in turn manufactures finished products. This symbiotic relationship enhances the economic well-being of both trading partners and fosters global economic interdependence.

Moreover, international sales promote cultural exchange and understanding, as goods from different regions bring unique aspects of their originating cultures to new markets. This exchange is not limited to physical goods but also includes ideas, traditions, and innovations embedded within these products. For instance, the export of traditional crafts from one country can introduce foreign consumers to new artistic techniques and cultural heritage, fostering a greater appreciation for diversity. Similarly, the global distribution of technological products can disseminate cutting-edge innovations, encouraging worldwide technological advancement and collaboration.

Furthermore, the sale of goods is critical for the survival and growth of businesses, particularly small and medium-sized enterprises (SMEs). Engaging in international trade allows these businesses to access larger markets, increase their customer base, and achieve economies of scale. This can lead to higher revenues, increased investment in innovation, and the creation of new jobs. For SMEs, the ability to participate in international trade can be a transformative opportunity, enabling them to compete on a global stage and contribute to economic development in their home countries.

The legal frameworks and principles governing the sale of goods play a vital role in ensuring the predictability and security of international transactions. These frameworks provide clear rules for contract formation, performance, and enforcement, reducing the uncertainties and risks associated with cross-border trade. They also offer mechanisms for resolving disputes, which is crucial for maintaining business relationships and ensuring that trade disputes do not escalate into larger conflicts. By providing a stable and predictable legal environment, these frameworks encourage businesses to engage in international trade, thereby supporting global economic growth and integration.

Key Principles and Concepts ..

The key principles governing the sale of goods include the transfer of ownership, risk allocation, and the obligations of the parties involved. These principles are designed to provide clarity and predictability in commercial transactions, minimizing disputes and enhancing trade efficiency. The contractual obligations typically involve the delivery of goods, payment of the price, and compliance with terms agreed upon by the parties. Understanding these principles is essential for navigating the complexities of international sales and ensuring compliance with legal standards. These principles form the bedrock of commercial transactions and their effective application ensures smooth and dispute-free operations in the global marketplace.

One fundamental concept is the transfer of ownership, which determines when and how the ownership of goods shifts from the seller to the buyer. This transfer often occurs when the goods are delivered or when the contract terms specify. The moment of transfer is critical as it defines the point at which the buyer assumes control and ownership of the goods. This concept is closely linked to the idea of insurable interest, as the party with ownership typically has the right to insure the goods against loss or damage. Variations in the point of ownership transfer can significantly impact the legal and financial responsibilities of the involved parties.

Another critical concept is risk allocation, which addresses who bears the risk of loss or damage to the goods at different stages of the transaction. Clear risk allocation helps prevent disputes and ensures that both parties are aware of their responsibilities. Typically, the risk transfers from the seller to the buyer either when the goods are delivered or when they are handed over to the carrier. This principle ensures that the parties can accurately assess their potential liabilities and make informed decisions about insurance and other protective measures. For instance, under Incoterms like FOB (Free on Board), the risk shifts when goods pass the ship's rail, while under CIF (Cost, Insurance, and Freight), the seller retains the risk until the goods reach the destination port.

The obligations of the parties involved in the sale of goods also play a crucial role in defining the contours of commercial transactions. The seller's primary obligation is to deliver the goods in accordance with the contract terms, which includes ensuring that the goods are of the agreed quantity, quality, and description. The buyer's principal obligation is to accept and pay for the goods as specified in the contract. These obligations are further detailed in various international instruments, such as the CISG, which outline the rights and duties of buyers and sellers, including the inspection of goods, notice of non-conformity, and the right to claim remedies in case of breach. Adherence to these obligations ensures the smooth execution of contracts and fosters trust between trading partners.

In addition to these fundamental principles, various legal doctrines and practices underpin the sale of goods, including the doctrine of privity of contract and the concept of good faith. The privity of contract doctrine establishes that only parties to the contract are bound by and can enforce its terms, ensuring that contractual rights and obligations are clearly defined and limited to the contracting parties. The principle of good faith, often implied in commercial contracts, requires parties to act honestly and fairly in the execution of their contractual duties. This principle helps maintain ethical standards in trade and mitigates the potential for opportunistic behavior that could undermine commercial relationships. These concepts collectively create a robust legal framework that supports the integrity and reliability of international sales transactions.

TOPIC 1:

The United Nations Convention on Contracts for the International Sale of Goods (CISG)

Overview and Historical Context

The United Nations Convention on Contracts for the International Sale of Goods (CISG), adopted in 1980, stands as a cornerstone in the harmonization of international sales law. It aims to provide a consistent and uniform legal framework for the international sale of goods, thereby reducing the legal barriers that historically hampered cross-border trade. By establishing clear and universally applicable rules, the CISG seeks to enhance predictability and legal certainty in international transactions, fostering a more conducive environment for global commerce. With its adoption by numerous countries, the CISG now governs a significant portion of global trade, underscoring its pivotal role in the contemporary international legal landscape.

The historical context of the CISG's development is rooted in the complexities and inefficiencies that characterized international sales law prior to its adoption. Before the CISG, international sales transactions were subject to a myriad of national laws, creating a patchwork of regulations that often led to confusion and increased transaction costs. Businesses engaged in cross-border trade faced significant legal uncertainties, as they had to navigate diverse and sometimes conflicting legal systems. This fragmented legal environment not only heightened the risks and costs associated with international trade but also acted as a deterrent to smaller enterprises looking to enter the global market. The need for a cohesive and standardized legal framework became increasingly apparent as international trade expanded.

The impetus for the creation of the CISG came from the United Nations Commission on International Trade Law (UNCITRAL), which recognized the necessity of a unified legal framework to facilitate smoother international transactions. UNCITRAL's efforts culminated in the drafting of the CISG, which was designed to be a self-contained legal instrument, offering a comprehensive set of rules for the formation, performance, and enforcement of international sales contracts. The CISG sought to balance the interests of both buyers and sellers, providing equitable solutions that could be universally accepted. This balanced approach has been a key factor in its widespread adoption and success.

One of the critical achievements of the CISG is its ability to transcend the diverse legal traditions and commercial practices of different countries. By providing a neutral and internationally accepted set of rules, the CISG mitigates the disadvantages that can arise from the application of domestic laws in cross-border transactions. This neutrality is particularly important in international trade, where parties often come from vastly different legal and cultural backgrounds. The CISG's provisions, which address fundamental aspects of contract law such as offer and acceptance, obligations of the parties, and remedies for breach, are crafted to be clear and straightforward, reducing the potential for disputes and misunderstandings.

Despite its many advantages, the CISG has not been without its criticisms and challenges. Some critics argue that the CISG's provisions are too general and lack the specificity needed to address certain complex commercial scenarios. Others point out that variations in the interpretation and application of the CISG by different national courts can lead to inconsistencies, undermining its goal of uniformity. Moreover, not all countries have adopted the CISG, and significant trading nations, such as the United Kingdom, remain outside its purview. This partial adoption limits the CISG's effectiveness in creating a truly global legal framework for international sales. Nonetheless, the CISG remains a critical tool in the arsenal of international trade law, continually evolving and adapting to meet the needs of the global trading community.

Scope and Application

The United Nations Convention on Contracts for the International Sale of Goods (CISG) serves as a critical tool for harmonizing international sales law, applying to contracts for the sale of goods between parties whose places of business are in different states, provided these states are contracting parties to the CISG or the contract specifies its application. The CISG, however, delineates its boundaries by explicitly excluding certain types of sales. These exclusions include sales involving consumer goods, auctions, securities, ships, and aircraft, and electricity, ensuring the convention's provisions are primarily focused on commercial transactions. The comprehensive scope of the CISG encompasses the formation of contracts, the rights and obligations of the parties involved, and remedies for breach of contract. Through these provisions, the CISG aims to balance the interests of both buyers and sellers, fostering fairness and predictability in international trade.

One of the key benefits of the CISG is its ability to reduce the complexity and uncertainty that often accompany international sales transactions. Without a uniform legal framework, parties to a contract must navigate the intricate web of varying national laws, which can lead to unpredictable legal outcomes and increased transaction costs. By providing a standardized set of rules, the CISG mitigates these issues, enabling businesses to plan and execute international sales with greater confidence. This uniformity is particularly valuable for small and medium-sized enterprises (SMEs) that may lack the resources to manage complex legal environments. The CISG's broad scope and detailed provisions offer a comprehensive framework that addresses many of the common issues arising in international sales, such as contract formation, delivery obligations, and remedies for breach.

The application of the CISG begins with the formation of the contract. The convention provides clear guidelines on what constitutes an offer and an acceptance, crucial elements for determining the existence of a contract. According to the CISG, an offer is a proposal for concluding a contract that is sufficiently definite and indicates the intention of the offeror to be bound in case of acceptance. An acceptance is a statement or conduct by the offeree indicating assent to the offer. These provisions ensure that the process of contract formation is clear and predictable, reducing the risk of disputes over whether a valid contract has been formed. Furthermore, the CISG addresses the issue of modifications to contracts, allowing for flexibility while maintaining legal certainty.

The rights and obligations of the parties under the CISG are designed to ensure a fair balance between buyers and sellers. For sellers, the primary obligations include delivering the goods, handing over any documents related to them, and ensuring that the goods conform to the contract. For buyers, the main obligations are to pay the price for the goods and take delivery of them. These provisions are intended to reflect common commercial practices and provide a clear framework for the performance of international sales contracts. The CISG also includes detailed rules on the inspection of goods, which allow buyers to verify that the goods meet the contractual specifications. This inspection must be conducted within a reasonable time after delivery, ensuring that any issues are identified and addressed promptly.

Remedies for breach of contract under the CISG are another critical aspect of its scope. The convention provides a range of remedies that aim to be fair and equitable, reflecting the nature of the breach and the circumstances of the case. For instance, if the seller fails to deliver the goods or delivers non-conforming goods, the buyer can require performance, claim damages, or, in certain cases, avoid the contract. Similarly, if the buyer fails to pay the price or take delivery, the seller can require performance, claim damages, or avoid the contract. These remedies are designed to provide effective recourse for the aggrieved party while promoting the resolution of disputes in a manner that preserves the contractual relationship where possible.

Despite its broad applicability, the CISG is not without limitations and challenges. One significant limitation is the exclusion of certain types of sales, such as consumer goods, which means that the CISG primarily governs commercial transactions. This exclusion is based on the recognition that consumer transactions often involve different legal considerations and protections than commercial sales. Additionally, the CISG does not apply automatically in all international sales contracts; it applies only if both parties are from contracting states or if the contract explicitly incorporates its provisions. This requirement can lead to situations where the CISG's uniform rules do not apply, leaving parties to navigate the complexities of national laws.

Another challenge associated with the CISG is the potential for variations in interpretation and application by national courts. While the CISG aims to provide a uniform legal framework, the interpretation of its provisions can vary depending on the legal traditions and practices of different countries. This can lead to inconsistencies in how the CISG is applied, potentially undermining its goal of legal predictability. To mitigate this issue, efforts have been made to promote a consistent interpretation of the CISG, including the publication of case law and scholarly commentary that provide guidance on its application.

The CISG's provisions on risk allocation are also noteworthy. The convention specifies that the risk of loss or damage to the goods passes from the seller to the buyer at a specific point in the transaction. This point can vary depending on the terms of the contract, such as whether the contract involves the carriage of goods. The clear allocation of risk is crucial for managing the uncertainties associated with international trade, ensuring that both parties are aware of their responsibilities and can take appropriate measures to protect their interests. The CISG's rules on risk allocation are designed to reflect common commercial practices and provide a fair balance between the interests of buyers and sellers.

In addition to its substantive provisions, the CISG also includes rules on its own scope and application. For example, the CISG applies to sales contracts between parties whose places of business are in different contracting states, provided that the contract does not explicitly exclude its application. This territorial scope ensures that the CISG governs a wide range of international sales transactions, promoting the harmonization of sales law across different jurisdictions. However, the CISG also allows parties to opt out of its provisions, providing flexibility for parties who prefer to apply a different legal framework to their contract.

In conclusion, the scope and application of the CISG encompass a comprehensive range of issues related to international sales contracts, including contract formation, rights and obligations, and remedies for breach. By providing a uniform legal framework, the CISG reduces the complexity and uncertainty associated with international sales, promoting fairness and predictability in global trade. However, the CISG is not without its limitations and challenges, including its exclusion of certain types of sales and the potential for variations in interpretation. Despite these challenges, the CISG remains a vital tool for harmonizing international sales law and facilitating cross-border commerce.

Key Provisions and Principles

The United Nations Convention on Contracts for the International Sale of Goods (CISG) is structured around several key provisions and principles that are designed to facilitate international trade by providing a uniform and predictable legal framework. These provisions cover crucial aspects of contract formation, the obligations of the parties involved, and the remedies available for breach of contract. Each of these areas is addressed with an emphasis on fairness, efficiency, and the commercial realities of cross-border transactions.

Contract Formation (Articles 14-24): The CISG offers a comprehensive framework for the formation of contracts, which is essential for ensuring that parties have a clear understanding of their rights and obligations. Articles 14-24 detail the rules governing offers, acceptances, and the moment a contract is considered to be formed. An offer under the CISG must be sufficiently definite and indicate the offeror's intention to be bound in case of acceptance. An acceptance, meanwhile, must be an unequivocal assent to the terms of the offer. The convention also addresses the timing of acceptances and the concept of "battle of the forms," where conflicting terms in exchanged documents are reconciled.

The CISG's approach to contract formation is notably flexible, accommodating various forms of communication and recognizing the dynamic nature of international trade. For instance, it allows for contracts to be formed through informal communications such as emails or oral agreements, provided the necessary elements of offer and acceptance are present. This flexibility helps to reduce misunderstandings and disputes about whether a contract has been validly formed, thus promoting smoother commercial interactions.

Seller's Obligations (Articles 30-44): The obligations of the seller under the CISG are outlined in Articles 30-44. These articles stipulate that the seller must deliver the goods, hand over any documents related to them, and ensure that the goods conform to the terms of the contract. The delivery must occur within the agreed time frame, and the goods must be of the quantity, quality, and description required by the contract. Additionally, the goods must be properly packaged and fit for any particular purpose made known to the seller at the time of the contract formation.

The emphasis on conformity and delivery underscores the CISG's focus on the performance of contractual duties in good faith. This approach is intended to align the expectations of the buyer and the seller, reducing the likelihood of disputes. Furthermore, the provisions require that the seller inform the buyer about any potential risks related to the goods, thus promoting transparency and trust in international trade.

Buyer's Obligations (Articles 53-65): Articles 53-65 define the obligations of the buyer, primarily focusing on the payment of the price and the taking of delivery. The buyer must pay the price in accordance with the contract and any applicable trade terms, and take all necessary steps to facilitate the transfer of the goods. This includes ensuring that any required import licenses or permits are obtained. The buyer must also inspect the goods within a reasonable time after delivery and notify the seller of any non-conformities.

The obligations of the buyer under the CISG highlight the reciprocal nature of international sales contracts. By requiring prompt inspection and notification of non-conformities, the CISG aims to resolve potential issues swiftly, thereby minimizing disruption to the commercial relationship. This promptness also ensures that sellers can address any defects without unnecessary delays, which is crucial in maintaining the integrity of international supply chains.

Remedies for Breach (Articles 74-77): The CISG provides a robust set of remedies for breach of contract, aiming to preserve the economic balance of the agreement and ensure that the injured party is adequately compensated. Articles 74-77 outline the remedies available, which include damages, specific performance, and contract avoidance. Damages under the CISG are intended to cover the loss suffered by the injured party, including any lost profits, provided that the damages were foreseeable at the time the contract was concluded.

The principle of foreseeability is critical in the CISG's damages regime, as it aligns the compensation with the expectations of the parties at the time of contracting. This approach helps to ensure that damages are fair and proportionate, reflecting the actual economic impact of the breach. Additionally, the option of specific performance allows the injured party to demand the fulfillment of contractual obligations, which can be particularly important in cases where monetary compensation is insufficient.

Avoidance of Contract (Articles 49 and 64): The CISG also addresses the conditions under which a contract can be avoided. Articles 49 and 64 allow for contract avoidance in cases of fundamental breach, where the breach substantially deprives the other party of what they were entitled to expect under the contract. The right to avoid the contract is an essential remedy, as it allows the injured party to terminate the contractual relationship and seek alternative arrangements without being bound by the breached contract.

Fundamental breach, as defined by the CISG, emphasizes the severity of the breach and its impact on the injured party. This provision ensures that avoidance is reserved for significant violations, thus maintaining the stability of contractual relationships while providing a necessary exit mechanism in cases of serious non-performance. The requirement for timely notice of avoidance further underscores the importance of clarity and decisiveness in managing contract disputes.

Inspection and Notice (Articles 38-39): Articles 38 and 39 of the CISG require the buyer to inspect the goods within a reasonable time after delivery and notify the seller of any lack of conformity. Failure to do so within a reasonable period can result in the buyer losing the right to rely on the non-conformity. This provision aims to strike a balance between the interests of both parties by ensuring that any issues are identified and addressed promptly, preventing prolonged uncertainty and potential losses.

The inspection and notice requirements promote efficiency and fairness in international sales transactions. By encouraging prompt identification and notification of defects, these provisions help to minimize the impact of non-conformities on the buyer's business operations. They also protect sellers from unfounded claims long after the goods have been delivered, thus providing a clear timeframe for resolving disputes.

Interest on Sums in Arrears (Article 78): Article 78 of the CISG stipulates that if a party fails to pay the price or any other sum that is in arrears, the other party is entitled to interest on that sum. The rate of interest is not specified in the CISG, allowing it to be determined based on the applicable national law or the terms agreed upon by the parties. This provision ensures that the non-breaching party is compensated for the time value of money, reflecting the economic realities of delayed payments.

The entitlement to interest serves as a deterrent against late payments and reinforces the importance of timely performance in international sales transactions. By compensating the injured party for the delay, Article 78 helps to maintain the financial equilibrium of the contract and encourages adherence to payment obligations.

Mitigation of Loss (Article 77): Article 77 imposes a duty on the injured party to take reasonable measures to mitigate the loss resulting from the breach. This duty aligns with the principle of fairness by ensuring that the non-breaching party does not exacerbate their losses unnecessarily. If the injured party fails to mitigate their loss, the breaching party can seek a reduction in the damages owed.

The mitigation requirement promotes responsible behavior and economic efficiency in the resolution of contract disputes. By encouraging the injured party to take proactive steps to minimize their losses, Article 77 helps to ensure that damages are limited to the actual harm caused by the breach, thereby fostering a balanced approach to compensation.

Good Faith and Fair Dealing: Although not explicitly stated in a specific article, the principles of good faith and fair dealing underpin the entire CISG framework. These principles require parties to act honestly and fairly in the performance and enforcement of their contractual obligations. The emphasis on good faith reflects the CISG's commitment to fostering trust and cooperation in international trade.

The principles of good faith and fair dealing serve as a guiding ethos for interpreting and applying the provisions of the CISG. They provide a normative foundation that supports the convention's objective of promoting fair and equitable trade practices. By embedding these principles in the CISG, the convention aligns legal obligations with the ethical standards of international commerce.

Conclusion: The key provisions and principles of the CISG provide a comprehensive and balanced framework for governing international sales contracts. By addressing critical aspects such as contract formation, obligations of the parties, and remedies for breach, the CISG promotes fairness, predictability, and efficiency in international trade. Its flexibility and emphasis on commercial realities make it an indispensable tool for businesses engaged in cross-border transactions. However, the effectiveness of the CISG also depends on consistent interpretation and application by national courts, highlighting the ongoing need for legal harmonization and international cooperation.

Case Law and Interpretation

Case law under the United Nations Convention on Contracts for the International Sale of Goods (CISG) is pivotal in interpreting its provisions and ensuring their consistent application across jurisdictions. As an international treaty, the CISG aims to provide a uniform legal framework for the sale of goods, reducing legal barriers and fostering predictability in international trade. The body of jurisprudence that has developed around the CISG is instrumental in clarifying ambiguous terms and addressing novel issues, thereby enhancing the convention's effectiveness and reliability.

Role of Case Law in Clarifying Provisions

One of the critical functions of case law under the CISG is to elucidate ambiguous terms and fill gaps in the convention's text. Given the general nature of many CISG provisions, courts and arbitral tribunals have the task of interpreting these provisions in the context of specific disputes. This interpretative role is essential because it ensures that the CISG remains flexible and adaptable to various commercial practices and legal traditions.

For example, the interpretation of "fundamental breach" under Article 25 of the CISG has been a subject of significant judicial analysis. Courts have grappled with defining what constitutes a breach that "substantially deprives" the aggrieved party of what they are entitled to expect under the contract. Decisions from various jurisdictions have contributed to a more nuanced understanding of this concept, balancing the need for contractual stability with the protection of parties' expectations.

Uniform Application and Legal Certainty

The development of a coherent body of case law is vital for the uniform application of the CISG. Divergent interpretations can undermine the convention's goal of providing a standardized legal framework. Therefore, courts and tribunals often look to foreign decisions to ensure consistency. The principle of uniformity, enshrined in Article 7(1) of the CISG, obligates courts to consider the international character of the convention and the need to promote uniform application.

One illustrative case is the decision of the "Oberlandesgericht" (OLG) Hamburg in the "Caviar Case" (2005), where the court considered the interpretation of "reasonable time" under Article 39(1) for notifying the seller of a lack of conformity. The court referred to decisions from other jurisdictions to establish a consistent standard, highlighting the importance of international jurisprudence in promoting uniform application.

Practical Issues and Business Guidance

Case law under the CISG also addresses practical issues that arise in the course of international sales transactions, providing valuable guidance for businesses and legal practitioners. For instance, the determination of damages under Articles 74-77 has been extensively litigated, with courts elucidating the scope and limitations of recoverable damages, including lost profits and mitigation efforts.

In the "Iron Molybdenum Case" (BGH, Germany, 1999), the German Federal Court of Justice provided a detailed analysis of the calculation of damages, including the foreseeability of losses under Article 74. This case clarified that damages must be a foreseeable consequence of the breach at the time of contract formation, thus offering crucial insights for businesses in assessing potential liabilities and risks.

Handling Non-Conforming Goods

The issue of non-conforming goods is another area where CISG case law has made significant contributions. Articles 35-44 of the CISG outline the seller's obligations regarding the conformity of goods, but disputes often arise over what constitutes a breach of these obligations and the appropriate remedies.

In the "Frozen Pork Case" (Austrian Supreme Court, 2008), the court addressed the criteria for determining non-conformity under Article 35, emphasizing the relevance of contract specifications and the reasonable expectations of the buyer. This decision underscored the importance of clear contractual terms and provided guidance on assessing conformity in line with commercial standards.

Interpretation Across Jurisdictions

The CISG's global adoption necessitates that courts consider the convention's international character and strive for interpretations that align with its underlying principles. This cross-jurisdictional perspective is crucial for maintaining the CISG's uniform application and ensuring that its provisions are interpreted consistently worldwide.

For example, the decision in the "Chilean Grapes Case" (Supreme Court of the Netherlands, 2002) highlighted the importance of looking at foreign judgments. The Dutch court examined interpretations from various jurisdictions to resolve issues related to the timeliness of notification of non-conformity, demonstrating a commitment to international coherence in CISG jurisprudence.

Impact on Global Trade

The growing body of case law under the CISG significantly impacts global trade by providing predictability and legal certainty. Businesses engaged in international sales can rely on this jurisprudence to understand their rights and obligations better, reducing the risk of disputes and fostering a stable commercial environment.

Legal scholars and practitioners closely analyze CISG case law to stay abreast of evolving interpretations and their implications for international trade. The continuous development of case law ensures that the CISG remains relevant and responsive to the needs of global commerce, adapting to new challenges and commercial practices.

Challenges in Harmonization

Despite the progress made in developing a coherent body of CISG case law, challenges remain in achieving complete harmonization. Differences in legal culture, judicial interpretation, and procedural rules can lead to varying applications of the CISG across jurisdictions. These discrepancies can undermine the convention's goal of uniformity and necessitate ongoing efforts to promote harmonized interpretations.

For instance, the interpretation of "good faith" under Article 7(1) has varied, with some courts adopting a broad, substantive interpretation while others apply it more narrowly. Addressing these interpretative differences is crucial for ensuring that the CISG's principles are consistently applied and respected globally.

Role of Scholarly Commentary

Scholarly commentary plays a vital role in the development and interpretation of CISG case law. Legal scholars analyze court decisions, identify trends, and provide critical insights that help shape future interpretations. This academic input is invaluable for practitioners and judges seeking to navigate complex legal issues under the CISG.

The collaborative efforts of academia, the judiciary, and the legal profession contribute to a deeper understanding of the CISG and its application, fostering a well-rounded and informed body of jurisprudence. This synergy between theory and practice enhances the convention's effectiveness and ensures that it evolves in line with commercial realities.

Conclusion

The critical role of case law in interpreting and applying the CISG cannot be overstated. Through judicial decisions and arbitral awards, the provisions of the CISG are clarified, refined, and adapted to address the practicalities of international trade. This evolving body of jurisprudence ensures that the CISG remains a robust and reliable framework for governing international sales of goods, promoting legal certainty and predictability in global commerce. However, the quest for uniformity continues to require diligent efforts from courts, arbitrators, and scholars to harmonize interpretations and uphold the convention's core principles.

TOPIC 2:

QUESTION:

The 1980 United Nations Convention on Contracts for the International Sale of Goods (CISG) and the Common Law . *Is There a Problem?*

Comparison of CISG and Common Law Principles

The CISG and common law systems, particularly those of English-speaking countries, differ significantly in their approach to contract law. The CISG emphasizes a uniform set of rules designed to facilitate international trade, whereas common law systems are based on judicial precedents and case-specific interpretations. Key differences include the treatment of contract formation, the parol evidence rule, and the concept of fundamental breach. For instance, the CISG adopts a more flexible approach to contract formation and interpretation, allowing for greater consideration of the parties' intentions and commercial practices.

Contract Formation

Under the CISG, the formation of a contract is more flexible compared to the rigid structure of common law systems. Articles 14-24 of the CISG outline the requirements for offer and acceptance, emphasizing the importance of intent and the actual behavior of the parties involved. The CISG does not require a specific form for a contract to be valid, allowing for oral agreements and considering practices established between the parties or usages in international trade.

In contrast, common law systems, such as those in the United States and the United Kingdom, adhere to a more stringent set of rules for contract formation. A clear offer and unequivocal acceptance are fundamental, and any variation from the terms of the offer typically constitutes a counteroffer rather than acceptance. This strict approach can sometimes lead to the failure of contract formation over minor discrepancies, a problem less likely under the CISG's more lenient framework.

The Parol Evidence Rule

The parol evidence rule in common law jurisdictions prohibits the introduction of evidence outside the written contract to alter or add to its terms, assuming the contract is intended to be a complete and final representation of the parties' agreement. This rule aims to preserve the integrity of written agreements and prevent fraud and perjury in contract disputes. However, it can also lead to rigid interpretations that exclude relevant contextual information.

The CISG, however, takes a more inclusive approach. Article 8 of the CISG allows for consideration of all relevant circumstances, including pre-contractual negotiations, practices established between the parties, and subsequent conduct. This holistic method acknowledges the complexity of international transactions and strives to ensure that the true intent of the parties is honored, even if it means deviating from the written document.

Fundamental Breach

The concept of fundamental breach also differs notably between the CISG and common law systems. Under Article 25 of the CISG, a breach is considered fundamental if it results in such detriment to the other party as substantially to deprive him of what he is entitled to expect under the contract. This definition is inherently flexible, taking into account the expectations and actual losses of the parties.

In contrast, common law systems generally categorize breaches more rigidly. The distinction between conditions and warranties in common law dictates the remedies available. A breach of a condition allows for termination of the contract and damages, whereas a breach of a warranty typically permits only damages. This strict categorization can sometimes fail to adequately address the nuances of the breach's impact on the contractual relationship.

Contract Interpretation

Interpretation of contracts under the CISG involves a broader perspective, emphasizing the parties' intentions and the context in which the contract was formed. Article 7(1) of the CISG mandates that the convention should be interpreted with regard to its international character and the need to promote uniformity and good faith in international trade. This approach allows for a more nuanced understanding of contractual terms and fosters consistency across different jurisdictions.

Common law interpretation, on the other hand, tends to be more literal and text-based. Courts focus primarily on the plain meaning of the words used in the contract, with less emphasis on external factors or the broader context. This can lead to interpretations that strictly adhere to the written terms, potentially overlooking the parties' actual intentions or commercial realities.

Remedies for Breach

The remedies available under the CISG and common law systems also exhibit significant differences. The CISG offers a range of remedies for breach of contract, including specific performance, damages, and contract avoidance. Article 46 of the CISG, for example, allows the buyer to require the seller to perform his obligations, provided this is not unreasonable under the circumstances. This emphasis on performance aligns with the goal of maintaining the contractual relationship whenever possible.

In common law jurisdictions, specific performance is considered an equitable remedy and is granted only in exceptional circumstances where damages are deemed inadequate. The preference is generally for monetary compensation to put the injured party in the position they would have been in had the contract been performed. This approach reflects a more adversarial stance, prioritizing compensation over the continuation of the contractual relationship.

Good Faith

The principle of good faith is explicitly recognized in the CISG but is often implicit or applied differently in common law systems. Article 7(1) of the CISG requires that in interpreting the convention, regard is to be had to its international character and the need to promote the observance of good faith in international trade. This provision underlines the importance of fair dealing and honest conduct in fulfilling contractual obligations.

In common law, good faith is not uniformly applied and varies significantly across jurisdictions. In the United States, for example, the Uniform Commercial Code (UCC) includes a duty of good faith in the performance and enforcement of contracts. However, English law traditionally does not recognize a general duty of good faith, though recent developments suggest a gradual shift towards acknowledging its importance in certain contexts. This divergence highlights the more principle-based nature of the CISG compared to the rule-based structure of common law.

Role of Precedent

Precedent plays a pivotal role in common law systems, where past judicial decisions inform the interpretation and application of the law. This reliance on case law creates a body of jurisprudence that evolves over time, providing guidance and predictability. However, it can also lead to rigidities and complexities, as courts must navigate an extensive history of precedents.

The CISG, in contrast, aims for a more uniform and codified approach, reducing the reliance on precedent. While case law under the CISG is important for interpreting its provisions, the focus is on promoting uniformity and consistency across different jurisdictions. This difference underscores the CISG's goal of creating a cohesive international legal framework, as opposed to the more fragmented and evolving nature of common law jurisprudence.

Practical Implications for Businesses

For businesses engaged in international trade, understanding the differences between the CISG and common law principles is crucial. The CISG's flexible and inclusive approach can be advantageous in facilitating smoother transactions and reducing disputes. Its provisions on contract formation, interpretation, and remedies offer a predictable and balanced framework that accommodates the complexities of international commerce.

However, businesses operating under common law systems may find the stricter rules and precedents beneficial for their clarity and stability. The well-established body of case law provides a comprehensive guide for navigating contractual disputes, although it may sometimes lead to more rigid outcomes. The choice of legal framework can significantly impact contractual negotiations, dispute resolution, and overall commercial strategy.

Harmonization Efforts

Efforts to harmonize international commercial law have focused on bridging the gaps between the CISG and common law principles. Organizations like the United Nations Commission on International Trade Law (UNCITRAL) continue to develop guidelines and model laws that encourage the adoption of uniform standards. These initiatives aim to create a more cohesive global legal environment, facilitating international trade and reducing legal uncertainties.

Harmonization efforts face challenges, particularly in reconciling the different legal traditions and practices. The common law's reliance on precedent and detailed procedural rules contrasts with the CISG's principle-based approach. Achieving a balance between these systems requires ongoing dialogue and cooperation among legal scholars, practitioners, and international bodies. The goal is to create a legal framework that supports the dynamic nature of global trade while respecting the diversity of national legal systems.

Conclusion

The comparison between the CISG and common law principles reveals both significant differences and opportunities for convergence. While the CISG offers a flexible and uniform framework suited to the needs of international trade, common law systems provide stability and detailed guidance through their reliance on precedent. Understanding these differences is essential for businesses, legal practitioners, and policymakers engaged in the global marketplace. By recognizing the strengths and limitations of each system, stakeholders can navigate the complexities of international sales contracts more effectively and contribute to the ongoing harmonization of international commercial law.

TOPIC 3:

Challenges and Criticisms

Despite its many advantages, the CISG faces a number of significant challenges and criticisms. One major issue is the lack of awareness and understanding among legal practitioners. This lack of familiarity can lead to inconsistent application and misinterpretation of its provisions. In some jurisdictions, lawyers and judges may default to domestic law principles even when the CISG should apply, undermining the uniformity that the CISG seeks to promote.

Furthermore, the CISG has been criticized for its vagueness in certain areas. Its provisions are intentionally broad and flexible to accommodate the diverse commercial practices across different legal systems. However, this flexibility can also lead to significant uncertainty. For example, terms such as "reasonable time" and "fundamental breach" are open to interpretation, which can result in inconsistent judgments across different jurisdictions. This vagueness requires a nuanced understanding and often leads to divergent applications, complicating the predictability that international businesses seek.

Another challenge arises from the interplay between the CISG and domestic laws. In common law jurisdictions, established legal principles and doctrines may conflict with the CISG's provisions.

For instance, the common law parol evidence rule, which restricts the use of outside evidence in interpreting written contracts, contrasts sharply with the CISG's more permissive stance on considering pre-contractual negotiations. These conflicts can create legal uncertainties, as practitioners and courts may struggle with which rules to apply in specific situations, potentially leading to increased litigation and inconsistency.

The issue of "opt-outs" also presents a challenge. The CISG allows parties to exclude its application or derogate from or vary the effect of any of its provisions. While this flexibility is intended to respect party autonomy, it can undermine the convention's goal of uniformity. If parties frequently opt out of the CISG or modify its provisions, the resulting contracts may reflect a patchwork of CISG and domestic law elements, reducing the predictability and consistency that the CISG aims to provide.

Moreover, the enforcement of CISG provisions can be problematic. Different courts may interpret and apply the CISG's provisions in varied ways, leading to inconsistent outcomes. This inconsistency can be particularly pronounced in countries with less developed legal systems, where judicial interpretation of international treaties may be less sophisticated or experienced.

This disparity underscores the need for more comprehensive training and education on the CISG for judges and lawyers worldwide.

Additionally, there is a concern that the CISG does not adequately address the realities of modern international trade, particularly with respect to digital commerce. The CISG was drafted in the pre-digital era, and while it has been broadly effective, its provisions do not explicitly cover issues related to electronic contracts, digital signatures, and online transactions. This gap requires supplementary legal frameworks or updated provisions to ensure that the CISG remains relevant in the context of 21st-century commerce.

The CISG's provisions on remedies also face scrutiny. While the convention aims to balance the interests of buyers and sellers, some critics argue that it does not always provide adequate remedies for breaches. For example, the requirement for a fundamental breach to justify contract avoidance can be a high threshold to meet, potentially leaving aggrieved parties with insufficient recourse. Additionally, the CISG's emphasis on specific performance as a remedy, which is less common in some legal systems, can lead to enforcement challenges.

Another area of criticism is the CISG's limited scope. It explicitly excludes certain types of sales, such as consumer goods and auction sales, which means it does not cover all international sales transactions. This exclusion limits its applicability and leaves gaps that must be filled by other legal frameworks. Critics argue that expanding the scope of the CISG could enhance its effectiveness and provide a more comprehensive legal regime for international sales.

The CISG's implementation can also vary significantly between different countries. While over 90 countries have adopted the CISG, the extent to which it is integrated into domestic legal systems can differ. Some countries may have fully embraced the CISG, incorporating its principles into national law and judicial practice, while others may have adopted it more superficially, leading to uneven application and enforcement.

In conclusion, while the CISG has significantly advanced the harmonization of international sales law, it is not without its challenges and criticisms. Addressing these issues requires continued efforts in education, harmonization, and potential updates to the convention to ensure that it remains effective and relevant. Enhanced training for legal practitioners and judges, increased awareness among businesses, and ongoing dialogue between legal systems are crucial steps towards overcoming these challenges and maximizing the CISG's benefits in international trade.

Encyclopedia   - **THE PATRON** -   .100

TOPIC 4:

Harmonization Efforts and Future Prospects

Marwan M. Alarjan   - **MASTR** -   Martin Apollo Bureau

Efforts to harmonize the CISG with domestic laws and other international instruments are critical for reducing legal uncertainties and enhancing the convention's effectiveness. Harmonization aims to create a cohesive legal framework that can be consistently applied across different jurisdictions, thereby fostering greater predictability and stability in international trade. Such efforts are multifaceted, involving legislative reforms, judicial training, and the development of interpretive guidance to address ambiguities in the CISG's provisions.

One of the primary methods for promoting harmonization is through the creation of educational programs and resources targeted at legal practitioners, businesses, and academics. These programs aim to increase awareness and understanding of the CISG, ensuring that it is applied consistently and effectively. Workshops, seminars, and online courses can provide practical training on the CISG's application, while academic research can offer deeper insights into its provisions and their implications.

The role of international legal bodies such as UNCITRAL and the International Chamber of Commerce (ICC) is crucial in these harmonization efforts. These organizations can facilitate dialogue between national governments and legal practitioners, promoting the exchange of best practices and the development of interpretive guidance. UNCITRAL, for instance, has published a digest of CISG case law, which provides a comprehensive analysis of judicial decisions and helps to clarify the convention's provisions.

National governments also play a key role in harmonizing the CISG with domestic laws. Legislative reforms can be enacted to align national legal frameworks with the CISG's principles, ensuring that the convention is fully integrated into domestic law. This process may involve amending existing statutes or enacting new legislation that explicitly incorporates the CISG. Additionally, governments can encourage the judiciary to consider international case law and interpretive guidance when applying the CISG, promoting a more uniform approach.

Judicial training is another important aspect of harmonization efforts. Judges need to be familiar with the CISG and its application to ensure that it is interpreted consistently across different jurisdictions. Training programs can provide judges with the necessary knowledge and skills to apply the CISG effectively, including guidance on how to address ambiguities and reconcile conflicts between the CISG and domestic law.

Harmonization also involves collaboration with trade organizations and businesses to ensure that the CISG meets the practical needs of international trade. Trade organizations can provide valuable feedback on the CISG's provisions and their impact on commercial practices, helping to identify areas where further refinement is needed. Businesses, in turn, can benefit from a more predictable and stable legal environment, which can reduce transaction costs and facilitate cross-border trade.

Future prospects for the CISG include increased adoption by additional countries, further extending its reach and impact. As more countries adopt the CISG, the benefits of harmonization will become more pronounced, creating a more cohesive and predictable legal framework for international sales. This increased adoption will also contribute to the development of a more comprehensive body of case law, which can provide further clarity and guidance on the CISG's application.

Interpretive guidance will continue to play a crucial role in refining the CISG's provisions and addressing ambiguities. International legal bodies and national governments can collaborate to develop interpretive tools that help to clarify the convention's provisions and promote their uniform application.

This may include the publication of commentaries, guidelines, and model contracts that provide practical guidance on the CISG's application.

The development of electronic commerce and digital trade presents new challenges and opportunities for the CISG. As international trade increasingly moves online, there is a need to ensure that the CISG remains relevant and applicable to digital transactions. This may involve updating the CISG's provisions to address issues related to electronic contracts, digital signatures, and online dispute resolution. Future prospects for the CISG include adapting to these technological advancements and ensuring that it continues to provide a robust legal framework for international sales.

Sustainable development and corporate social responsibility (CSR) are also emerging areas of focus for the CISG. There is growing recognition that international trade should be conducted in a manner that promotes environmental sustainability and respects human rights. The CISG can play a role in this by incorporating provisions that encourage sustainable practices and CSR in international sales. This could involve developing guidelines on sustainable sourcing, fair labor practices, and environmental protection, helping to ensure that international trade contributes to broader social and environmental goals.

In conclusion, ongoing harmonization efforts and future prospects for the CISG are essential for enhancing its effectiveness and promoting its wider acceptance and application. Continued collaboration among international legal bodies, national governments, and trade organizations is crucial for addressing the challenges facing the CISG and ensuring that it remains relevant in a rapidly changing global trade environment. By fostering greater awareness, providing interpretive guidance, and adapting to new developments, the CISG can continue to serve as a cornerstone of international commercial law, facilitating smoother and more predictable cross-border transactions.

TOPIC 5:

Key Contracts in International Sales

FOB (Free on Board) Contract

FOB (Free on Board) contracts are a cornerstone of maritime trade, providing a clear delineation of responsibilities between buyers and sellers. In an FOB contract, the seller's obligations are fulfilled once the goods pass the ship's rail at the designated port of shipment. From that point forward, the buyer assumes all risks and costs associated with the goods. This division of responsibilities has significant implications for the logistics, risk management, and financial arrangements in international sales.

The fundamental principle of the FOB contract is the clear transfer of risk from seller to buyer at a specific point—the ship's rail. This transfer point is critical because it defines when and where the seller's responsibility ends and the buyer's begins. By establishing this precise moment, FOB contracts provide certainty and clarity, which are essential for managing the complex logistics of international shipping. For sellers, this means their responsibility for the goods is limited to ensuring they are properly loaded onto the vessel. Once this is accomplished, the seller can relinquish control and focus on other aspects of their business, knowing that any subsequent risks are borne by the buyer.

For buyers, an FOB contract requires careful planning and coordination. Since the risk and cost of transportation, insurance, and any potential damages or losses transfer to the buyer once the goods are on board, the buyer must arrange for shipping and insurance from the port of shipment to the final destination. This responsibility necessitates a thorough understanding of international shipping logistics and insurance markets. Buyers must ensure that they have reliable shipping partners and comprehensive insurance coverage to mitigate the risks associated with transporting goods across international waters.

One of the main advantages of FOB contracts is the cost efficiency for sellers. By transferring the responsibility for transportation and insurance to the buyer, sellers can avoid the complexities and potential costs associated with these logistics. This can be particularly advantageous for small and medium-sized enterprises (SMEs) that may lack the resources and expertise to manage international shipping. However, this benefit for sellers translates into additional burdens for buyers, who must bear the costs and risks associated with the transportation of goods from the port of shipment.

FOB contracts also promote transparency and accountability in international trade. The clear delineation of responsibilities helps prevent disputes related to transportation and risk management. Since both parties understand their obligations and the point at which risk transfers, there is less room for misunderstandings and conflicts. This transparency is further enhanced by the use of standardized trade terms, such as those defined by the International Chamber of Commerce (ICC) in Incoterms, which provide a common language and set of rules for international trade.

However, FOB contracts are not without their challenges. One of the main criticisms is the potential for disputes over the exact moment when the goods pass the ship's rail. In practice, this can be a contentious issue, especially if there are delays or problems with loading the goods onto the vessel. Discrepancies in documentation, such as bills of lading, can also complicate matters, leading to disputes over whether the seller has fulfilled their obligations. To mitigate these risks, it is essential for both parties to maintain clear and accurate records and to communicate effectively throughout the shipping process.

Another challenge associated with FOB contracts is the complexity of managing transportation and insurance for buyers. For businesses that lack experience in international shipping, this can be a daunting task. Buyers must navigate a range of logistical issues, from selecting reliable shipping companies to negotiating insurance policies that provide adequate coverage. The financial burden of these responsibilities can be significant, particularly for SMEs. Additionally, buyers must be prepared to handle any issues that arise during transit, such as delays, damage, or loss of goods.

Despite these challenges, FOB contracts remain a popular choice in international trade due to their clear allocation of responsibilities and risks. They are particularly well-suited to industries where maritime shipping is the primary mode of transportation, such as the bulk commodities and manufacturing sectors. By providing a straightforward framework for the transfer of risk and cost, FOB contracts facilitate efficient and effective trade relationships.

The legal framework supporting FOB contracts is robust and well-established. The principles underlying FOB contracts are recognized in various international legal instruments, including the Uniform Commercial Code (UCC) in the United States and the United Nations Convention on Contracts for the International Sale of Goods (CISG). These legal frameworks provide additional clarity and support for parties engaged in FOB transactions, ensuring that their rights and obligations are protected.

In conclusion, FOB contracts are a critical tool in international trade, offering clear benefits in terms of risk management and cost efficiency. While they present certain challenges, particularly for buyers, their advantages in providing clarity and transparency make them a preferred choice for many businesses engaged in maritime trade. As international trade continues to evolve, FOB contracts will remain an essential component of the global commercial landscape, facilitating the efficient and predictable movement of goods across borders. For businesses, understanding the intricacies of FOB contracts and effectively managing their associated responsibilities is crucial for success in the international marketplace.

CIF (Cost, Insurance, and Freight) Contract

A CIF (Cost, Insurance, and Freight) contract is a type of international sales agreement where the seller assumes multiple responsibilities that extend beyond merely delivering the goods. In a CIF contract, the seller is obligated to place the goods on board the vessel, cover the costs of transport to the destination port, and procure insurance to protect the goods during transit. The transfer of risk occurs when the goods pass the ship's rail at the port of shipment, which distinguishes CIF from other types of international sales contracts like FOB (Free on Board).

One of the primary advantages of CIF contracts is the inclusion of insurance, which offers protection for the buyer against various risks that may occur during transit. This insurance coverage is typically arranged by the seller, ensuring that the buyer receives compensation in case of loss or damage to the goods while they are in transit. This aspect of CIF contracts provides an added layer of security for the buyer, making it a preferred choice for transactions involving high-value goods or shipments to regions with higher risks.

By covering the cost of freight, CIF contracts simplify the logistical process for the buyer. The seller arranges and pays for the transportation of the goods to the destination port, which can significantly reduce the logistical burden on the buyer. This is particularly advantageous for buyers who may lack the resources or expertise to manage complex international shipping arrangements. The seller's responsibility to deliver the goods to the destination port ensures that the buyer receives the goods without having to navigate the intricacies of international freight logistics.

The clarity in defining the obligations of both parties is another key benefit of CIF contracts. By specifying that the seller must deliver the goods on board the vessel, pay for transportation, and obtain insurance, CIF contracts provide a clear framework that minimizes misunderstandings and disputes. This clarity is crucial for maintaining smooth and efficient trade relationships, as it ensures that both parties are aware of their responsibilities and can plan accordingly.

Despite these advantages, CIF contracts also have their challenges. One potential issue is the determination of the insurance coverage. The insurance procured by the seller must be sufficient to cover the value of the goods and any potential risks during transit. However, disagreements can arise if the buyer feels that the insurance coverage is inadequate or does not meet their specific requirements. To mitigate this risk, it is important for both parties to agree on the level of insurance coverage and the terms of the insurance policy before finalizing the contract.

Another challenge with CIF contracts is the point of risk transfer. While the seller bears the cost of transportation and insurance until the goods reach the destination port, the risk of loss or damage passes to the buyer once the goods pass the ship's rail at the port of shipment. This means that the buyer assumes the risk during the actual sea voyage, despite the seller arranging the freight and insurance. Buyers must be aware of this risk transfer and ensure that the insurance coverage provided by the seller adequately protects their interests.

Additionally, CIF contracts can sometimes lead to disputes over the quality and condition of the goods upon arrival. Since the buyer assumes the risk during the sea voyage, any damage or deterioration that occurs during transit can result in disagreements. To address this issue, it is essential for the buyer to conduct thorough inspections upon receipt of the goods and to promptly notify the seller and the insurance company of any issues. Clear documentation and communication are key to resolving such disputes efficiently.

From a seller's perspective, CIF contracts require a greater level of involvement and responsibility compared to other contract types, such as FOB. The seller must manage the logistics of shipping, secure appropriate insurance, and ensure that the goods are delivered to the destination port. This can be resource-intensive and may require a higher level of expertise in international trade and logistics. However, for sellers with the necessary capabilities, CIF contracts can provide a competitive advantage by offering a comprehensive service to buyers.

For international trade practitioners, understanding the nuances of CIF contracts is crucial for navigating the complexities of global commerce. Legal professionals and trade experts must be well-versed in the specific obligations and risks associated with CIF contracts to advise their clients effectively. This includes ensuring that all contractual terms are clearly defined, that appropriate insurance coverage is in place, and that both parties understand the point of risk transfer.

In conclusion, CIF contracts offer significant benefits in terms of simplicity, clarity, and risk management, making them a popular choice in international trade. By covering the cost of freight and insurance, CIF contracts reduce the logistical burden on buyers and provide protection against transit risks. However, they also present challenges related to insurance adequacy, risk transfer, and potential disputes over goods' condition. Both buyers and sellers must navigate these challenges carefully to ensure successful and mutually beneficial trade transactions. Understanding the intricacies of CIF contracts and effectively managing the associated responsibilities is essential for thriving in the global marketplace.

C&F (Cost and Freight) Contract

In a Cost and Freight (C&F) contract, the seller assumes responsibility for delivering the goods on board the vessel and covering the transportation costs to the destination port. Unlike Cost, Insurance, and Freight (CIF) contracts, the seller does not arrange for insurance under C&F terms. The risk transfers to the buyer once the goods pass the ship's rail at the port of shipment. This nuanced difference significantly impacts the distribution of responsibilities and risks between the buyer and the seller, positioning C&F contracts as an intermediary option between Free on Board (FOB) and CIF contracts.

C&F contracts offer certain logistical advantages for the seller, as the primary obligation is to ensure that the goods are loaded onto the vessel and transported to the destination port. By not being required to procure insurance, the seller's administrative burden is reduced. This can streamline the transaction process, making it more straightforward for sellers to manage their logistics operations. However, the absence of seller-arranged insurance necessitates that buyers take a proactive role in ensuring the goods are insured, introducing a layer of complexity for the buyer.

One significant advantage for buyers under C&F contracts is the flexibility to arrange their own insurance coverage. Buyers might prefer this option if they have access to more favorable insurance rates or have specific requirements for coverage that the seller might not provide under a CIF contract. This flexibility can lead to cost savings and better-aligned risk management strategies for the buyer, who can tailor the insurance to their precise needs.

Despite these benefits, the transfer of risk at the port of shipment introduces considerable responsibility for the buyer. From the moment the goods pass the ship's rail, the buyer bears all risks associated with the transportation of the goods, including damage or loss during the voyage. This necessitates careful selection of shipping companies and diligent management of insurance policies to mitigate these risks effectively. Buyers must ensure that the coverage is adequate and that they understand the claims process in case of any issues during transit.

For sellers, C&F contracts can be appealing due to the reduced liability and lower operational complexity compared to CIF contracts. By not being responsible for insurance, sellers can focus more on their core activities, such as production and logistics. However, they must ensure that the goods are delivered to the ship in good condition and comply with all contractual terms to avoid potential disputes and liabilities before the risk transfers to the buyer.

One of the critical challenges in C&F contracts is the potential for disputes over the condition of goods upon arrival at the destination port. Since the risk is transferred at the port of shipment, any damage that occurs during transit falls under the buyer's responsibility. To mitigate this, buyers must conduct thorough inspections upon receipt and promptly notify both the seller and the insurance company of any discrepancies. Clear documentation, including photos and reports from independent inspectors, can be crucial in supporting claims and resolving disputes.

Additionally, C&F contracts require clear communication and understanding between the parties to ensure that all terms and conditions are agreed upon and met. The lack of seller-provided insurance means that buyers and sellers must explicitly outline their responsibilities regarding the transport and handling of goods. Any ambiguities in the contract can lead to misunderstandings and potential conflicts, underscoring the importance of detailed and precise contractual terms.

The dynamic nature of international trade means that C&F contracts must also adapt to various legal and regulatory environments. Different jurisdictions may have specific requirements or interpretations of C&F terms, which can affect the enforcement and execution of contracts. Legal practitioners and trade professionals must stay informed about these differences to provide accurate guidance and ensure compliance with local and international laws.

From an economic perspective, C&F contracts can influence the pricing and competitiveness of goods in the international market. Sellers might offer more competitive prices under C&F terms since they are not bearing the cost of insurance. Buyers, on the other hand, can leverage their ability to negotiate better insurance rates to manage overall costs. This interplay can affect market dynamics and the decision-making process for both buyers and sellers when choosing the appropriate contract terms.

In conclusion, C&F contracts represent a balanced approach to managing the responsibilities and risks associated with international sales. By delineating the seller's obligation to deliver and transport goods without including insurance, these contracts offer flexibility and cost benefits, particularly for buyers who can secure favorable insurance terms. However, the transfer of risk at the port of shipment places significant responsibility on the buyer, necessitating careful risk management and proactive engagement in the shipping and insurance processes. Clear communication, detailed contracts, and a thorough understanding of the legal and regulatory landscape are essential for successfully navigating C&F agreements in international trade.

FAS (Free Alongside Ship) Contract

An FAS (Free Alongside Ship) contract is a specific type of shipping agreement used in international trade, wherein the seller's responsibility is to deliver the goods alongside the vessel at the designated port of shipment. From that point onward, the buyer assumes all risks and costs, including loading the goods onto the vessel and subsequent transportation. This type of contract is particularly prevalent in the trade of bulk commodities, such as agricultural products, minerals, and chemicals, where large quantities of goods are involved.

One of the primary advantages of an FAS contract is the flexibility it offers to buyers. By assuming responsibility for loading and transportation, buyers can exert greater control over the logistics process. This control can be beneficial for buyers with specific logistical requirements or those who can secure more favorable rates for loading and transportation services. For example, a buyer with established relationships with local port operators or shipping companies may be able to negotiate better terms than the seller, resulting in cost savings.

However, this flexibility also places significant responsibility on the buyer. The buyer must ensure that all arrangements for loading and transportation are in place, including securing the necessary equipment and labor to load the goods onto the vessel. This can be particularly challenging in busy ports or where specialized handling equipment is required. The buyer must also ensure that all necessary documentation, such as export licenses and customs declarations, is in order to avoid delays and additional costs.

The clear delineation of responsibility at the point where the goods are placed alongside the ship is a crucial aspect of FAS contracts. This clarity helps to prevent misunderstandings and disputes between the buyer and seller. Both parties know exactly when the transfer of risk occurs, which can aid in managing expectations and planning logistics. For sellers, this means that their risk is limited to delivering the goods to the designated port, after which any issues related to loading or transportation fall to the buyer.

Despite these advantages, FAS contracts can present challenges, particularly in terms of coordination and communication. The buyer must coordinate closely with the seller to ensure that the goods are delivered at the correct time and place, ready for loading onto the vessel. Any miscommunication or delays can result in increased costs or missed shipping deadlines, which can have significant implications for international trade. Therefore, clear communication and detailed planning are essential to the successful execution of FAS contracts.

Moreover, the requirement for the buyer to handle the loading process introduces additional risks. Loading goods onto a vessel is a complex operation that requires careful planning and execution to avoid damage to the goods or the vessel. Buyers must have the necessary expertise and resources to manage this process effectively. Inexperienced buyers may find themselves facing unexpected challenges and costs, which can negate the potential cost savings of an FAS contract.

The legal implications of FAS contracts also need to be considered. Since the buyer assumes risk once the goods are placed alongside the ship, any damage or loss occurring during loading or subsequent transportation is the buyer's responsibility. This can lead to disputes if there is any ambiguity about when the transfer of risk occurred or if the goods were damaged before being placed alongside the ship. Legal frameworks and international conventions, such as the Incoterms® rules published by the International Chamber of Commerce (ICC), provide guidelines to help mitigate these issues, but clear contract terms are essential.

In terms of insurance, the buyer must arrange for coverage from the point the goods are placed alongside the ship. This differs from CIF (Cost, Insurance, and Freight) contracts, where the seller arranges for insurance up to the destination port. Buyers must ensure that their insurance policies adequately cover the risks associated with loading and transportation. Failure to do so can result in significant financial losses if the goods are damaged or lost.

FAS contracts are also influenced by the specific terms and conditions agreed upon between the buyer and seller. Detailed contract terms can help to manage risks and ensure that both parties are clear about their responsibilities. These terms should include specifications for the timing and location of delivery, the condition of the goods, and the procedures for handling disputes. Effective contract management is crucial to the successful implementation of FAS contracts.

In summary, FAS contracts offer significant benefits in terms of flexibility and control for buyers, but they also introduce substantial responsibilities and risks. Buyers must be well-prepared to handle the logistical challenges and legal implications associated with loading and transporting goods. Clear communication, detailed planning, and comprehensive contract terms are essential to managing these risks and ensuring successful international trade transactions under FAS terms. For sellers, FAS contracts provide a clear endpoint for their responsibilities, but they must still ensure timely and accurate delivery to the designated port. Overall, FAS contracts can be a valuable tool in international trade, provided that both parties fully understand and manage their respective obligations and risks.

TOPIC 6:

Definitions and Obligations Under Each Contract

FOB (Free on Board) Contract

In an FOB (Free on Board) contract, the seller's obligations are met once the goods pass the ship's rail at the designated port of shipment. This means that the seller is responsible for all costs and risks associated with transporting the goods to the port and loading them onto the vessel. The buyer assumes all risks and costs from that point forward, including shipping, insurance, and any other expenses incurred until the goods reach their final destination. This division of responsibilities provides a clear cut-off point, making it easier for both parties to manage their respective obligations.

The clear delineation of responsibilities in an FOB contract is beneficial for sellers, as their liability ends once the goods are on board the ship. This can simplify logistics and financial planning for the seller. However, the buyer must be prepared to handle all subsequent risks, including arranging for shipping and insurance. This can be a disadvantage for buyers who are not experienced in managing these logistics or who may face higher costs for shipping and insurance than the seller.

CIF (Cost, Insurance, and Freight) Contract

A CIF (Cost, Insurance, and Freight) contract places additional obligations on the seller compared to an FOB contract. The seller must not only deliver the goods on board the vessel but also pay for the cost of transporting the goods to the destination port and arrange for insurance coverage during transit. The risk transfers to the buyer once the goods pass the ship's rail at the port of shipment, similar to an FOB contract. However, the inclusion of insurance in a CIF contract provides additional security for the buyer.

CIF contracts are advantageous for buyers, especially those who may not have the expertise or resources to arrange for shipping and insurance themselves. The seller's responsibility to arrange for these services can simplify the transaction for the buyer and reduce the risk of shipping-related issues. However, CIF contracts can also lead to higher costs for the buyer, as the seller may include a markup on the shipping and insurance costs.

C&F (Cost and Freight) Contract

A C&F (Cost and Freight) contract is similar to a CIF contract but without the obligation for the seller to arrange for insurance. Under a C&F contract, the seller must deliver the goods on board the vessel and pay for the cost of transport to the destination port. The risk transfers to the buyer once the goods pass the ship's rail at the port of shipment. The buyer is responsible for arranging and paying for insurance from that point onward.

C&F contracts offer a middle ground between FOB and CIF contracts. They simplify logistics for the seller, similar to an FOB contract, but also provide some of the cost-covering benefits of a CIF contract. This arrangement can be advantageous for buyers who prefer to manage their own insurance coverage, potentially securing better rates or more comprehensive policies than those arranged by the seller. However, it also requires the buyer to take on the responsibility and risk of insuring the goods during transit.

FAS (Free Alongside Ship) Contract

In an FAS (Free Alongside Ship) contract, the seller's responsibility is to place the goods alongside the vessel at the designated port of shipment. The buyer assumes all risks and costs from that point onward, including loading the goods onto the vessel, shipping, and insurance. This type of contract is often used for bulk commodities and emphasizes the buyer's control over the loading and transportation process.

FAS contracts can be advantageous for buyers who have specific logistical requirements or who can negotiate better rates for loading and transportation services. By assuming responsibility for these aspects of the shipment, the buyer can exert greater control over the logistics and potentially reduce costs. However, this arrangement also places significant responsibility on the buyer, requiring them to manage the logistics of loading the goods onto the vessel and ensuring all necessary documentation is in order.

Comparison and Implications

The definitions and obligations under each of these contract types provide a framework for managing international sales transactions. Each type of contract offers different benefits and challenges, depending on the needs and capabilities of the buyer and seller. FOB contracts are often preferred by sellers who want to limit their liability to the point of loading the goods onto the vessel. CIF contracts, on the other hand, are favored by buyers who want the security of knowing that shipping and insurance are arranged by the seller.

C&F contracts offer a compromise, allowing the seller to manage the cost of shipping while leaving the insurance responsibility to the buyer. FAS contracts provide the greatest flexibility for buyers in terms of managing logistics but also place the most responsibility on them. The choice of contract type depends on various factors, including the nature of the goods, the logistics capabilities of the buyer and seller, and the relative costs and risks involved.

Risk Management

Understanding the transfer of risk and cost responsibilities under each contract type is crucial for effective risk management. For example, in an FOB contract, the buyer must arrange for insurance coverage from the moment the goods are loaded onto the vessel. In a CIF contract, the seller arranges for insurance, but the buyer should still ensure that the coverage is adequate for their needs. C&F contracts require the buyer to take on the insurance responsibility, which can be both an advantage and a challenge, depending on their expertise in securing insurance.

Dispute Resolution

Clear definitions and obligations under each contract type help to minimize disputes by providing a framework for resolving issues. If a dispute arises, the specific terms of the contract can be referred to in order to determine which party is responsible for costs or risks at a given point in the transaction. This clarity is essential for maintaining good business relationships and ensuring that disputes are resolved efficiently and fairly.

Legal Considerations

The legal implications of each contract type must also be considered. Different jurisdictions may have specific requirements or interpretations of these contract terms, which can affect the enforcement of the contract. Parties must ensure that their contracts are drafted in compliance with relevant laws and that they fully understand the legal implications of the contract terms.

Conclusion

In conclusion, FOB, CIF, C&F, and FAS contracts each define specific obligations for the buyer and seller, providing a framework for managing international sales transactions. Understanding these definitions and obligations is crucial for drafting effective contracts and managing potential disputes. By clearly delineating the point at which risk and cost responsibilities transfer, these contracts help to ensure that transactions are conducted smoothly and efficiently, minimizing disputes and providing a framework for resolving any issues that may arise. This clarity and predictability are essential for successful international trade and the effective management of logistics and risks.

TOPIC 7:

Case Studies and Practical Considerations

CASE STUDIES:

Case studies and practical applications of FOB, CIF, C&F, and FAS contracts provide a tangible understanding of these contract types and their implications in real-world transactions. Analyzing specific cases helps illustrate the benefits and challenges associated with each contract type, offering practical guidance for businesses engaged in international sales. By examining detailed examples, businesses can gain insights into effectively managing risks and responsibilities in international trade.

Case Study 1: FOB Contract in Electronics Shipment

An electronics manufacturer in Japan enters into an FOB contract with a retailer in the United States for the shipment of high-value electronic devices. Under this contract, the manufacturer is responsible for delivering the goods on board the vessel at the port of Tokyo. Once the goods pass the ship's rail, the risk transfers to the buyer, who assumes all responsibilities for shipping, insurance, and further transportation to the destination.

In this case, the clear definition of the point of risk transfer is crucial. The manufacturer must ensure that the goods are safely loaded onto the vessel, and any damage or loss occurring during this process is their responsibility. The retailer, on the other hand, must arrange for insurance coverage from the moment the goods are on board. This scenario highlights the importance of understanding and managing the point of risk transfer to avoid disputes and ensure smooth transactions.

Case Study 2: CIF Contract for Agricultural Products

A South American agricultural exporter sells a large consignment of coffee beans to a European importer under a CIF contract. The exporter is responsible for delivering the coffee beans on board the vessel, paying for the cost of transport to the destination port in Hamburg, and obtaining insurance for the goods during transit. The risk transfers to the importer once the goods pass the ship's rail at the port of shipment.

This CIF contract provides the importer with significant advantages, including reduced logistical burden and the security of having insurance arranged by the exporter. However, the importer must ensure that the insurance coverage provided by the exporter is adequate. This case study demonstrates how CIF contracts can simplify logistics and provide additional security, but also underscores the need for importers to verify the sufficiency of the insurance coverage.

Case Study 3: C&F Contract for Industrial Machinery

A European manufacturer sells industrial machinery to a buyer in the Middle East under a C&F contract. The manufacturer is responsible for delivering the machinery on board the vessel and paying for the cost of transport to the destination port. Unlike CIF contracts, the manufacturer does not arrange for insurance. The risk transfers to the buyer once the goods pass the ship's rail at the port of shipment.

In this scenario, the buyer must arrange for insurance coverage from the moment the goods are loaded onto the vessel. This arrangement allows the buyer to potentially secure better insurance rates or more comprehensive coverage. However, it also places the responsibility for managing insurance on the buyer. This case study illustrates the trade-offs involved in C&F contracts, where the seller simplifies logistics, but the buyer takes on the insurance responsibility.

Case Study 4: FAS Contract for Bulk Commodities

A Canadian mining company sells bulk copper to an Asian buyer under an FAS contract. The mining company is responsible for placing the copper alongside the vessel at the port of Vancouver. The buyer assumes all risks and costs from that point onward, including loading the copper onto the vessel and arranging for shipping and insurance.

This FAS contract provides flexibility for the buyer, who can manage the loading and transportation according to their logistical preferences. However, it also places significant responsibility on the buyer to ensure that the loading process is conducted efficiently and safely. This case study highlights the importance of logistical coordination and the buyer's role in managing transportation and associated risks.

PRACTICAL CONSIDERATIONS:

1. **Nature of Goods:** The choice of contract type often depends on the nature of the goods being sold. High-value or perishable goods might benefit from CIF contracts, where the seller arranges for comprehensive insurance, while bulk commodities might be better suited to FAS contracts, allowing the buyer to manage loading and transportation logistics.

2. **Logistics Capabilities:** The logistical capabilities of the buyer and seller also influence the choice of contract. Sellers with well-established logistics networks might prefer FOB or CIF contracts to leverage their shipping and insurance arrangements, while buyers with specific logistical preferences might opt for FAS or C&F contracts.

3. **Cost and Risk Management:** Managing costs and risks is a critical consideration. Buyers and sellers must evaluate the cost implications of each contract type, including shipping and insurance costs, and balance these against the risks involved. For example, CIF contracts may result

in higher costs for the buyer due to the seller's markup on shipping and insurance.

4. **Legal and Regulatory Environment:** The legal and regulatory environment of the countries involved can impact the choice of contract type. Businesses must ensure that their contracts comply with relevant laws and regulations and consider any legal implications of the contract terms, such as the enforceability of insurance claims or dispute resolution mechanisms.

Conclusion

Analyzing case studies and practical applications of FOB, CIF, C&F, and FAS contracts provides valuable insights into their use in real-world transactions. Each contract type offers distinct advantages and challenges, depending on the nature of the goods, logistical capabilities, and cost and risk management considerations. By understanding these factors and examining detailed examples, businesses can make informed decisions on the appropriate contract type to effectively manage risks and responsibilities in international sales. This comprehensive understanding helps ensure smooth transactions, minimize disputes, and promote successful international trade relationships.

TOPIC 8:

The Favor of Choosing CIF Contract Rather than FOB Contract

Advantages of CIF Contracts:

Inclusion of Insurance: A Safety Net

One of the most significant advantages of CIF (Cost, Insurance, and Freight) contracts is the inclusion of insurance, which provides a safety net for the buyer against risks during transit. This feature ensures that the goods are protected from potential losses or damages that could occur while being transported. The insurance component of CIF contracts is particularly crucial for high-value or perishable goods, where any damage or loss could result in substantial financial losses. By securing insurance, the seller mitigates these risks for the buyer, providing a layer of security that is essential in international trade.

Simplified Logistics for Buyers

CIF contracts greatly simplify logistics for buyers. By covering the cost of freight and arranging for insurance, the seller takes on the responsibility of ensuring that the goods reach the destination port. This arrangement is especially beneficial for buyers who may lack the expertise or resources to manage complex transportation and insurance logistics. For small and medium-sized enterprises (SMEs) or businesses new to international trade, CIF contracts offer a hassle-free solution that allows them to focus on their core business operations rather than the intricacies of international shipping.

Cost Predictability and Financial Planning

The all-inclusive nature of CIF contracts provides cost predictability, which is a significant advantage for buyers. Since the seller assumes responsibility for freight and insurance costs, the buyer is spared from unexpected expenses that could arise from logistical mishaps. This cost predictability allows buyers to better manage their financial planning and budgeting, as they know the total cost upfront. In volatile markets where transportation costs can fluctuate, CIF contracts offer a stable and predictable financial framework.

Reduced Risk Exposure for Buyers

CIF contracts shift the risk exposure from buyers to sellers until the goods reach the port of destination. This transfer of risk is particularly beneficial in international trade, where the journey can involve multiple modes of transportation and potential hazards. By transferring risk at the port of shipment, buyers are protected from unforeseen events that could occur during transit, such as natural disasters, theft, or accidents. This risk mitigation is a compelling reason for buyers to prefer CIF contracts, especially when dealing with unfamiliar or high-risk shipping routes.

Enhanced Trust and Reliability

The inclusion of freight and insurance in CIF contracts enhances trust and reliability in the transaction. Buyers can be assured that the seller has a vested interest in ensuring the safe delivery of the goods, as any damage or loss would directly impact the seller's obligations. This built-in assurance fosters a more reliable and trustworthy trade relationship, reducing the likelihood of disputes and fostering long-term business partnerships. In an environment where trust is paramount, CIF contracts provide a solid foundation for confidence between trading partners.

Compliance with International Trade Norms

CIF contracts are widely recognized and accepted in international trade, complying with global standards and norms. This widespread acceptance facilitates smoother cross-border transactions, as both parties are likely to be familiar with the terms and conditions associated with CIF contracts. The standardized nature of CIF contracts reduces the potential for misunderstandings and legal disputes, promoting a more efficient and harmonious trading environment. This compliance with international norms is particularly advantageous for businesses operating in multiple countries, providing a consistent framework across different jurisdictions.

Flexibility and Negotiation Leverage

CIF contracts offer a degree of flexibility and negotiation leverage for both buyers and sellers. Sellers can use their knowledge and experience to secure favorable freight and insurance rates, which can then be passed on to buyers. Buyers, on the other hand, can negotiate terms that best suit their logistical and financial needs. This flexibility allows for tailored solutions that can optimize the benefits for both parties, making CIF contracts a versatile option in international trade.

Streamlined Dispute Resolution

The clarity and comprehensiveness of CIF contracts contribute to streamlined dispute resolution. Since the responsibilities and obligations of both parties are clearly defined, any disputes that arise can be resolved more efficiently. The inclusion of insurance also provides an additional layer of protection, as claims for damages or losses can be handled through the insurance policy. This streamlined approach to dispute resolution minimizes disruptions to the trade process and ensures that issues are addressed promptly and fairly.

Market Expansion Opportunities

By simplifying the logistics and reducing the risk exposure for buyers, CIF contracts enable businesses to expand their market reach. Companies can enter new international markets with greater confidence, knowing that the complexities of shipping and insurance are managed by the seller. This opportunity for market expansion can lead to increased sales, revenue growth, and enhanced competitiveness in the global marketplace. CIF contracts thus play a crucial role in facilitating international business growth and diversification.

Promoting Long-Term Business Relationships

CIF contracts promote long-term business relationships by fostering trust, reliability, and mutual benefits. The comprehensive nature of CIF contracts ensures that both parties have a clear understanding of their obligations and responsibilities, reducing the potential for conflicts. The built-in insurance and freight coverage also demonstrate a commitment to ensuring the safe delivery of goods, further strengthening the business relationship. Over time, this foundation of trust and reliability can lead to more significant collaboration, repeat business, and a stronger presence in the international market.

In conclusion, CIF contracts offer numerous advantages that make them an attractive option for international trade. The inclusion of insurance, simplified logistics, cost predictability, and reduced risk exposure are some of the key benefits that enhance the appeal of CIF contracts. Additionally, the promotion of trust, compliance with international norms, flexibility, streamlined dispute resolution, market expansion opportunities, and the fostering of long-term business relationships further underscore the value of CIF contracts. By understanding and leveraging these advantages, businesses can optimize their international trade operations and achieve greater success in the global marketplace.

Comparative Analysis with FOB Contracts:

1. Introduction to FOB and CIF Contracts

FOB (Free on Board) and CIF (Cost, Insurance, and Freight) contracts are two widely used terms in international trade, each with distinct implications for the allocation of risk, cost, and responsibility between the buyer and the seller. FOB contracts transfer the risk to the buyer once the goods pass the ship's rail at the port of shipment, while CIF contracts offer added protection by including insurance and covering transportation costs to the destination port. Understanding the nuances of these contract types is crucial for businesses engaged in cross-border transactions.

2. Risk Allocation

One of the primary differences between FOB and CIF contracts lies in risk allocation. Under an FOB contract, the risk of loss or damage to the goods transfers from the seller to the buyer once the goods pass the ship's rail at the port of shipment. This means that any incidents occurring during transit are the buyer's responsibility. In contrast, CIF contracts extend the seller's responsibility by including insurance coverage until the goods reach the destination port. This added protection under CIF contracts can be particularly valuable for buyers, especially when shipping high-value or fragile goods.

3. Transportation Responsibilities

FOB contracts place the onus of arranging and paying for transportation on the buyer once the goods are loaded onto the vessel. This can be advantageous for sellers, as their logistical responsibilities are minimized. However, it also means that buyers must have the expertise and resources to manage international shipping, which can be complex and costly. On the other hand, CIF contracts simplify logistics for the buyer by including the cost of freight to the destination port. This not only reduces the buyer's burden but also ensures a more seamless and coordinated shipping process.

4. Insurance Coverage

A critical advantage of CIF contracts over FOB contracts is the inclusion of insurance. Under a CIF contract, the seller is obligated to obtain marine insurance to cover the goods during transit, providing an additional layer of protection for the buyer. This insurance coverage ensures that any losses or damages incurred during shipping are compensated, giving buyers greater peace of mind. In contrast, FOB contracts leave the responsibility of arranging insurance to the buyer, who must secure appropriate coverage to mitigate risks.

5. Cost Implications

The cost implications of FOB and CIF contracts differ significantly. In an FOB contract, the buyer bears the cost of transportation and insurance from the port of shipment. This can lead to higher overall expenses for the buyer, particularly if they are not able to negotiate favorable shipping and insurance rates. Conversely, CIF contracts bundle these costs into the price paid to the seller, potentially offering cost savings due to the seller's ability to secure better rates. This can make CIF contracts more cost-effective for buyers, especially those with limited experience in international logistics.

6. Flexibility and Control

FOB contracts offer buyers greater flexibility and control over the shipping process. By managing transportation and insurance themselves, buyers can select carriers and insurers that best meet their needs and preferences. This level of control can be beneficial for buyers who require specific logistics solutions or have established relationships with shipping and insurance providers. In contrast, CIF contracts limit the buyer's control, as the seller arranges transportation and insurance. While this simplifies the process, it may not always align with the buyer's specific requirements.

7. Suitability for Different Types of Goods

The choice between FOB and CIF contracts can also depend on the nature of the goods being shipped. FOB contracts may be more suitable for goods that are less susceptible to damage and have lower transportation risks. Buyers of such goods might prefer FOB contracts for the flexibility and cost control they offer. Conversely, CIF contracts are often preferred for high-value, fragile, or perishable goods, where the added protection of insurance and the assurance of coordinated transportation are crucial. This comparative suitability underscores the importance of considering the specific characteristics of the goods in question.

8. Legal and Jurisdictional Considerations

Both FOB and CIF contracts are subject to different legal frameworks and interpretations depending on the jurisdictions involved. FOB contracts can sometimes lead to legal complexities, especially in determining the precise moment when risk transfers. This can result in disputes if the buyer and seller have different understandings of the contract terms. CIF contracts, with their clearly defined provisions for insurance and freight, tend to offer more straightforward legal interpretations, reducing the potential for disputes. However, it is essential for both parties to ensure that the contract terms comply with relevant international trade laws and regulations.

9. Case Study: Electronics Shipment under FOB Contract

Consider a case where an electronics company in the United States enters into an FOB contract with a manufacturer in China. Once the goods are loaded onto the ship in Shanghai, the risk transfers to the U.S. buyer. During transit, the goods are damaged due to rough seas. Under the FOB terms, the buyer must bear the cost of the damaged goods and manage the insurance claim. This scenario highlights the importance of buyers understanding their responsibilities under FOB contracts and securing adequate insurance coverage to protect their interests.

10. Case Study: Perishable Goods Shipment under CIF Contract

In another case, a European retailer imports fresh produce from South America under a CIF contract. The seller arranges transportation and insurance, ensuring the goods are protected during the long sea voyage. Upon arrival, the goods are found to be partially spoiled. The buyer can file a claim with the insurance company arranged by the seller, receiving compensation for the losses. This case demonstrates the advantage of CIF contracts for perishable goods, where insurance coverage is crucial for mitigating risks and ensuring financial protection.

11. Practical Considerations for Businesses

When deciding between FOB and CIF contracts, businesses must consider various practical factors, including their logistical capabilities, risk tolerance, and cost management strategies. Companies with robust logistics departments and experience in international shipping may prefer FOB contracts for the control and flexibility they offer. In contrast, businesses with limited resources or expertise may find CIF contracts more advantageous, as they simplify the shipping process and provide comprehensive protection.

12. Negotiation Dynamics

The negotiation dynamics between buyers and sellers can also influence the choice of contract. Sellers may prefer FOB contracts to limit their responsibilities and liabilities once the goods are shipped. Buyers, on the other hand, may negotiate for CIF terms to ensure the seller handles transportation and insurance. Effective negotiation requires a clear understanding of the trade-offs associated with each contract type and a focus on achieving a mutually beneficial agreement.

13. Impact on Trade Relationships

The choice between FOB and CIF contracts can impact the trade relationship between buyers and sellers. FOB contracts, with their clear delineation of responsibilities, can foster trust and clarity in the transaction. However, they may also lead to disputes if the transfer of risk and cost is not well understood. CIF contracts, by providing added protection and simplifying logistics, can strengthen the trade relationship by reducing the potential for conflict and ensuring smoother transactions.

14. Risk Management Strategies

Effective risk management is crucial in international trade, and the choice of contract plays a significant role in this. FOB contracts require buyers to implement robust risk management strategies, including securing appropriate insurance and managing transportation risks. CIF contracts, by incorporating insurance, provide a built-in risk management solution, which can be particularly valuable for businesses looking to mitigate risks without additional administrative burden.

15. Compliance with International Standards

Both FOB and CIF contracts are governed by international standards and regulations, such as the Incoterms published by the International Chamber of Commerce (ICC). These standards provide a common framework for interpreting contract terms and responsibilities, ensuring consistency and reducing the potential for disputes. Businesses must ensure that their contracts comply with these standards to facilitate smooth and legally sound transactions.

16. Training and Education for Practitioners

For businesses and legal practitioners, understanding the intricacies of FOB and CIF contracts is essential. Training and education programs can help practitioners navigate the complexities of these contracts, ensuring they can advise clients effectively and draft clear, comprehensive agreements. Ongoing professional development is crucial in keeping up with changes in international trade regulations and best practices.

17. Technological Advancements and Contract Management

Technological advancements, such as blockchain and digital contract management systems, are transforming the way FOB and CIF contracts are executed and managed. These technologies offer greater transparency, security, and efficiency in contract management, reducing the potential for disputes and streamlining the administrative processes involved in international trade. Businesses should explore these technological solutions to enhance their contract management capabilities.

18. Future Trends and Developments

The future of international trade contracts, including FOB and CIF terms, will likely be influenced by evolving trade dynamics, regulatory changes, and technological advancements. Emerging trends such as the increasing importance of sustainability and ethical considerations in trade may also impact contract terms and preferences. Staying informed about these trends and adapting contract strategies accordingly will be crucial for businesses to remain competitive in the global market.

19. Conclusion: Strategic Decision-Making

In conclusion, the choice between FOB and CIF contracts involves strategic decision-making based on a thorough understanding of the trade-offs and implications of each contract type. By carefully considering factors such as risk allocation, cost implications, logistical capabilities, and the nature of the goods, businesses can make informed decisions that align with their operational needs and strategic goals. Effective contract management and negotiation can enhance trade relationships and ensure successful international transactions.

20. Final Thoughts

Ultimately, both FOB and CIF contracts offer distinct advantages and challenges, and the choice between them should be tailored to the specific context of each transaction. By leveraging the strengths of each contract type and addressing potential pitfalls, businesses can optimize their international trade operations, manage risks effectively, and achieve their commercial objectives. Understanding the comparative analysis of these contracts is essential for any business engaged in global trade, providing a foundation for successful and sustainable international commerce.

Legal and Practical Considerations:

1. Introduction

The decision between CIF (Cost, Insurance, and Freight) and FOB (Free on Board) contracts is influenced by various legal and practical considerations. These include the nature of the goods, the logistical capabilities of the parties involved, and the specific requirements of the transaction. A deep understanding of the legal implications, including the allocation of risk and cost responsibilities, is crucial for drafting effective contracts and managing potential disputes.

2. Nature of the Goods

The nature of the goods being shipped is a significant factor in choosing between CIF and FOB contracts. For high-value or perishable goods, CIF contracts offer the advantage of insurance coverage, which provides protection against potential losses during transit. This can be crucial for goods that are susceptible to damage, as the insurance ensures compensation in case of unforeseen incidents. Conversely, for goods that are less valuable or less prone to damage, an FOB contract might suffice, allowing the buyer to save on the costs of insurance and freight.

3. Logistical Capabilities

The logistical capabilities of the buyer and seller are also crucial in determining the appropriate contract type. Buyers with established logistics departments and experience in managing international shipments may prefer FOB contracts, as these allow them greater control over transportation and insurance arrangements. On the other hand, sellers with extensive shipping networks and favorable shipping rates may prefer CIF contracts, as they can leverage their logistical strengths to manage transportation and insurance more effectively.

4. Specific Transaction Requirements

Each transaction has unique requirements that can influence the choice between CIF and FOB contracts. For instance, if the buyer requires timely and assured delivery of goods, a CIF contract may be preferable due to the seller's responsibility for transportation and insurance. This ensures that the goods are delivered to the destination port with minimal hassle for the buyer. In contrast, if the buyer needs to customize the shipping process or prefers to negotiate directly with carriers, an FOB contract might be more suitable.

5. Legal Implications: Allocation of Risk

Understanding the legal implications of risk allocation is essential in international trade. In an FOB contract, the risk transfers to the buyer once the goods pass the ship's rail at the port of shipment. This means the buyer is responsible for any loss or damage during transit. In contrast, under a CIF contract, the risk also transfers at the port of shipment, but the seller provides insurance to cover potential losses during transit. This allocation of risk affects how each party manages and mitigates their exposure to potential liabilities.

6. Cost Responsibilities

Cost responsibilities differ significantly between CIF and FOB contracts. In a CIF contract, the seller is responsible for the cost of transporting the goods to the destination port and obtaining insurance. This can simplify the transaction for the buyer, who only needs to handle the goods upon arrival. Conversely, an FOB contract requires the buyer to arrange and pay for transportation and insurance from the port of shipment, which can increase the buyer's costs and logistical burden but offers more control over these aspects.

7. Compliance with International Laws

International trade laws and regulations can impact the choice between CIF and FOB contracts. For example, certain countries may have specific legal requirements regarding the transportation and insurance of goods. Businesses must ensure that their contracts comply with these regulations to avoid legal disputes and penalties. Understanding the legal framework governing international trade is crucial for drafting compliant and effective contracts.

8. Minimizing Dispute Risks

Effective contract drafting is key to minimizing the risk of disputes. Clear definitions of responsibilities, risk allocation, and cost-sharing in CIF and FOB contracts help ensure that both parties understand their obligations. This clarity reduces the likelihood of misunderstandings and conflicts. Additionally, including detailed terms regarding dispute resolution mechanisms, such as arbitration or mediation, can provide a structured process for resolving any issues that arise.

9. Case Study: Perishable Goods in CIF Contracts

Consider a case where a food retailer in Europe imports fresh produce from South America under a CIF contract. The seller arranges transportation and insurance, ensuring that the perishable goods are covered during transit. Upon arrival, some of the produce is spoiled. The buyer can file a claim with the insurance company, arranged by the seller, to receive compensation for the spoiled goods. This case highlights the importance of CIF contracts for perishable goods, where insurance coverage is crucial for mitigating risks and ensuring financial protection.

10. Case Study: Electronics Shipment in FOB Contracts

In another case, a technology company in the United States sources electronic components from a manufacturer in China under an FOB contract. The buyer arranges transportation and insurance, taking responsibility for the goods once they pass the ship's rail in Shanghai. During transit, some components are damaged. The buyer must handle the insurance claim and manage the logistical complexities. This scenario demonstrates the need for buyers to understand their responsibilities under FOB contracts and secure appropriate insurance coverage to protect their interests.

11. Role of Insurance in CIF Contracts

Insurance is a critical component of CIF contracts, providing financial protection against risks during transit. By including insurance, CIF contracts offer a layer of security for the buyer, ensuring compensation for any losses or damages. This is particularly important for high-value or vulnerable goods, where the financial impact of damage or loss can be significant. The inclusion of insurance also simplifies the buyer's logistics, as the seller arranges coverage.

12. Control Over Logistics in FOB Contracts

FOB contracts offer buyers greater control over the logistics of transporting goods. This can be advantageous for buyers with established relationships with shipping companies or those who can negotiate better rates. By managing transportation and insurance independently, buyers can tailor the logistics to their specific needs and preferences. However, this control comes with increased responsibilities and potential risks, which buyers must be prepared to manage.

13. Practical Considerations for Drafting Contracts

When drafting CIF or FOB contracts, it is essential to include clear terms that define the responsibilities and obligations of each party. This includes specifying the point at which risk transfers, the parties responsible for transportation and insurance, and any other relevant terms. Detailed contract terms help ensure that both parties have a clear understanding of their roles, reducing the potential for disputes and misunderstandings.

14. Impact on Trade Relationships

The choice between CIF and FOB contracts can impact trade relationships. CIF contracts, by simplifying logistics and providing insurance, can foster trust and confidence between buyers and sellers. This arrangement can be particularly beneficial in new or developing trade relationships, where parties may seek to minimize risks. FOB contracts, while offering more control to buyers, require a higher level of trust and coordination between the parties to ensure smooth transactions.

15. Negotiation Dynamics

Negotiating CIF and FOB contracts involves balancing the interests and capabilities of both parties. Sellers may prefer CIF contracts to manage the logistics and ensure insurance coverage, while buyers may favor FOB contracts for the control they offer.

Effective negotiation requires a thorough understanding of the trade-offs and benefits of each contract type, as well as clear communication of each party's needs and preferences.

16. Legal Framework and Compliance

Compliance with international trade laws and regulations is essential for both CIF and FOB contracts. Businesses must ensure that their contracts align with the legal requirements of the countries involved in the transaction. This includes adhering to international standards, such as the Incoterms published by the International Chamber of Commerce (ICC), which provide guidelines for interpreting contract terms and responsibilities.

17. Training and Professional Development

For legal practitioners and business professionals, understanding CIF and FOB contracts is crucial for effective international trade operations. Ongoing training and professional development can help practitioners stay informed about changes in trade regulations and best practices. This knowledge enables them to draft clear and comprehensive contracts, advise clients effectively, and manage potential disputes.

18. Technological Advancements

Technological advancements, such as digital contract management systems and blockchain technology, are transforming the way CIF and FOB contracts are executed and managed. These technologies offer greater transparency, security, and efficiency in contract management, reducing the potential for disputes and streamlining administrative processes. Businesses should explore these technological solutions to enhance their contract management capabilities.

19. Future Trends and Developments

The future of CIF and FOB contracts will be influenced by evolving trade dynamics, regulatory changes, and technological advancements. Emerging trends such as sustainability and ethical considerations in trade may also impact contract terms and preferences. Staying informed about these trends and adapting contract strategies accordingly will be crucial for businesses to remain competitive in the global market.

20. Conclusion

In conclusion, the choice between CIF and FOB contracts involves a careful consideration of various legal and practical factors. By understanding the implications of risk allocation, cost responsibilities, logistical capabilities, and compliance with international laws, businesses can make informed decisions that align with their operational needs and strategic goals. Effective contract management and negotiation can enhance trade relationships, mitigate risks, and ensure successful international transactions.

Case Studies and Industry Preferences:

1. Introduction

Analyzing case studies and industry preferences provides valuable insights into the practical application of CIF (Cost, Insurance, and Freight) and FOB (Free on Board) contracts. These preferences vary across industries based on factors such as risk management, logistical capabilities, and specific transactional needs. This analysis will explore how different industries utilize CIF and FOB contracts, providing examples to illustrate their application.

2. The Shipping Industry and CIF Contracts

In the shipping industry, CIF contracts are often favored for the transportation of bulk commodities such as oil, grain, and minerals. The inclusion of insurance in CIF contracts offers significant advantages, particularly for commodities that are transported over long distances and exposed to various risks. For instance, a shipping company transporting crude oil from the

Middle East to Europe may prefer CIF contracts to ensure that the goods are insured against potential damages or losses during transit.

3. Bulk Commodities: Risk Management and Logistics

Bulk commodities present unique challenges in terms of risk management and logistics. CIF contracts simplify these challenges by transferring the responsibility for insurance and freight to the seller, who typically has better access to competitive shipping and insurance rates. This arrangement ensures that the goods are covered throughout the journey, providing peace of mind to the buyer who might lack the resources to manage these aspects independently.

4. Case Study: Oil Transportation

Consider a case study involving a European energy company importing crude oil from a Middle Eastern supplier. The supplier, experienced in handling large-scale shipments, arranges for the transport and insurance of the oil under a CIF contract. This setup allows the European company to focus on refining and distributing the oil without worrying about the complexities of international shipping and insurance, demonstrating the practical benefits of CIF contracts in the oil industry.

5. The Electronics Industry and FOB Contracts

In contrast, the electronics industry often favors FOB contracts, particularly for high-value goods like semiconductors, consumer electronics, and specialized components. These products require careful handling and timely delivery, and buyers in the electronics industry often prefer to manage logistics and insurance themselves to maintain control over these critical aspects.

6. High-Value Goods: Control and Customization

High-value goods necessitate precise logistical planning and risk management. FOB contracts provide buyers with the flexibility to select their preferred carriers and insurance providers, allowing for customization to meet specific requirements. For example, a tech company in the United States sourcing components from an Asian manufacturer might choose an FOB contract to ensure that the components are shipped under the strictest conditions to prevent damage or delays.

7. Case Study: Semiconductor Shipment

A tech giant in Silicon Valley sources semiconductors from a South Korean manufacturer under an FOB contract. The buyer arranges for specialized transportation and insurance, leveraging their established logistics network to ensure that the delicate semiconductors are handled with the utmost care. This control over the shipping process is crucial for maintaining the quality and reliability of the components, illustrating the benefits of FOB contracts in the electronics industry.

8. The Fashion Industry: A Mixed Approach

The fashion industry often employs both CIF and FOB contracts, depending on the nature of the goods and the preferences of the parties involved. For high-end fashion items, buyers may prefer CIF contracts to ensure that the goods are insured during transit, while for bulk shipments of lower-value items, FOB contracts might be used to leverage the buyer's logistical capabilities.

9. High-End Fashion: Ensuring Safe Transit

High-end fashion items, such as luxury clothing and accessories, require careful handling and insurance during transit. CIF contracts are advantageous in this context as they provide comprehensive coverage and reduce the buyer's logistical burden. For example, a European luxury brand importing handbags from an Italian manufacturer might opt for CIF contracts to ensure the products arrive in perfect condition.

10. Bulk Fashion Shipments: Cost-Effective Logistics

For bulk shipments of lower-value fashion items, FOB contracts can be more cost-effective. Retailers with extensive logistics networks may prefer to manage transportation and insurance themselves to optimize costs and streamline operations. This flexibility allows them to negotiate better rates and customize shipping arrangements to meet their specific needs.

11. Case Study: Luxury Handbags

A European luxury brand imports high-end handbags from an Italian manufacturer under a CIF contract. The manufacturer, experienced in exporting luxury goods, arranges for premium shipping and comprehensive insurance. This setup ensures that the handbags are protected against any potential damage during transit, maintaining the brand's reputation for quality and reliability.

12. Case Study: Mass-Market Apparel

A global fashion retailer sources mass-market apparel from multiple suppliers in Asia under FOB contracts. The retailer, with a sophisticated logistics operation, arranges for bulk shipping and insurance, taking advantage of economies of scale to reduce costs. This approach allows the retailer to maintain competitive pricing and manage large volumes of inventory efficiently.

13. The Automotive Industry: Managing Complexity

The automotive industry, characterized by complex supply chains and high-value components, often employs CIF contracts to manage risks associated with international shipping. Components such as engines, transmissions, and electronics are critical to the manufacturing process, and ensuring their safe delivery is paramount.

14. High-Value Components: Risk Mitigation

High-value automotive components require comprehensive insurance coverage to mitigate risks during transit. CIF contracts provide this assurance, ensuring that any losses or damages are covered. For example, an automaker in Germany sourcing engines from a supplier in Japan may use CIF contracts to ensure that the engines are insured and delivered on time.

15. Case Study: Engine Importation

A German automaker imports high-performance engines from a Japanese manufacturer under a CIF contract. The manufacturer arranges for specialized transportation and insurance, ensuring that the engines arrive safely. This arrangement reduces the logistical burden on the automaker and ensures that the production schedule remains on track.

16. The Pharmaceutical Industry: Ensuring Integrity

The pharmaceutical industry often relies on CIF contracts to ensure the integrity of sensitive products during transit. Pharmaceuticals require controlled environments and comprehensive insurance to protect against potential losses, making CIF contracts a preferred choice.

17. Sensitive Products: Controlled Environments

Pharmaceuticals, such as vaccines and biologics, require precise temperature control and handling during shipping. CIF contracts, which include insurance and freight, ensure that these sensitive products are transported under optimal conditions, reducing the risk of spoilage or damage.

18. Case Study: Vaccine Distribution

A global pharmaceutical company distributes vaccines from a production facility in Europe to various countries under CIF contracts. The company arranges for specialized refrigerated transport and comprehensive insurance, ensuring that the vaccines are delivered safely and effectively. This approach is critical for maintaining the efficacy of the vaccines and meeting regulatory requirements.

19. Industry Preferences and Contract Selection

Industry preferences for CIF or FOB contracts are influenced by several factors, including the value of the goods, the complexity of the logistics, and the risk management capabilities of the parties involved. Understanding these preferences and the practical considerations involved in selecting the appropriate contract type can help businesses optimize their international trade operations.

20. Conclusion

In conclusion, the choice between CIF and FOB contracts depends on various factors, including the nature of the goods, logistical capabilities, and industry preferences. Case studies from different industries illustrate the practical applications and benefits of each contract type. By understanding these considerations, businesses can make informed decisions that align with their operational needs and strategic goals, ensuring successful international transactions and effective risk management.

TOPIC 9:

Comparison with Other Legal Systems

Civil Law vs. Common Law Approaches:

1. Introduction to Civil Law and Common Law Systems

The international sale of goods necessitates navigating various legal systems, primarily civil law and common law. Civil law systems, such as those in Germany and France, rely on comprehensive legal codes that emphasize written statutes. Conversely, common law systems, prevalent in countries like the United States and the United Kingdom, are grounded in judicial precedents and case-specific interpretations. These foundational differences significantly impact the interpretation and application of international sales contracts, requiring a nuanced understanding of both legal traditions.

2. Historical Context and Evolution

Civil law systems originated from Roman law, particularly the Corpus Juris Civilis, and were further developed through the Napoleonic Code. These systems are characterized by their reliance on written statutes and comprehensive legal codes. Common law systems, on the other hand, evolved from English law and are distinguished by their reliance on judicial decisions and case law. The historical evolution of these systems has shaped their respective approaches to contract law, including the sale of goods.

3. Structure and Sources of Law

In civil law systems, the primary sources of law are legal codes and statutes, which provide detailed rules and guidelines. Judges in civil law jurisdictions apply these written laws to specific cases, with less emphasis on judicial interpretation. In common law systems, the primary sources of law include both statutes and case law. Judges play a significant role in interpreting and applying legal principles, creating a body of precedents that guide future decisions. This dual reliance on statutes and judicial decisions is a hallmark of common law systems.

4. Contract Formation in Civil Law

Civil law systems typically provide detailed statutory provisions on contract formation. These provisions outline the requirements for a valid contract, including offer, acceptance, and consideration. The emphasis is on ensuring that contracts are formed according to the prescribed legal formalities. This structured approach can provide greater predictability and certainty for parties entering into contracts for the sale of goods.

5. Contract Formation in Common Law

In common law systems, contract formation is governed by a combination of statutory provisions and judicial precedents. The requirements for a valid contract, such as offer, acceptance, and consideration, are defined through case law. This approach allows for greater flexibility, as courts can adapt legal principles to the specific circumstances of each case. However, it may also lead to less predictability, as the outcome can depend on judicial interpretation.

6. Interpretation of Contracts in Civil Law

Civil law systems prioritize the text of the contract and the intent of the parties as expressed in the written agreement. Judges focus on applying the statutory provisions to interpret contracts, with less emphasis on external evidence. This approach aims to provide clarity and reduce ambiguities by adhering closely to the written terms of the contract.

7. Interpretation of Contracts in Common Law

In common law systems, contract interpretation involves examining the language of the contract and the intent of the parties. Courts may consider extrinsic evidence, such as prior dealings and trade practices, to determine the parties' intentions. This broader approach allows for a more contextual interpretation of contracts but can introduce uncertainties due to the reliance on judicial discretion.

8. The Parol Evidence Rule

The parol evidence rule is a key principle in common law systems, which limits the use of external evidence to interpret written contracts. This rule aims to preserve the integrity of the written agreement by excluding evidence that contradicts or supplements the terms of the contract. In civil law systems, the focus is more on the written statutes and less on excluding external evidence, allowing for a more holistic interpretation of contracts.

9. Remedies for Breach of Contract in Civil Law

Civil law systems provide detailed statutory remedies for breach of contract, including specific performance, damages, and contract termination. These remedies are outlined in legal codes, offering clear guidance on the consequences of a breach. The structured nature of these remedies can provide certainty for parties seeking to enforce their contractual rights.

10. Remedies for Breach of Contract in Common Law

In common law systems, remedies for breach of contract are derived from both statutes and case law. Courts have broad discretion to award damages, specific performance, or other equitable remedies based on the circumstances of the case. This flexibility allows for tailored solutions but may also lead to variability in outcomes.

11. Case Study: Application of Civil Law in International Sales

A German manufacturer enters into a contract with a French retailer for the sale of machinery. The contract is governed by the German Civil Code (BGB), which provides detailed provisions on contract formation and performance. In the event of a dispute, the courts will apply the statutory provisions to interpret the contract and determine the appropriate remedies. This structured approach ensures that the parties have a clear understanding of their rights and obligations under the contract.

12. Case Study: Application of Common Law in International Sales

An American supplier contracts with a British buyer for the sale of software. The contract is governed by English common law, which relies on both statutory provisions and judicial precedents. In the event of a dispute, the courts will interpret the contract based on the language of the agreement and any relevant case law. The flexibility of the common law system allows the courts to consider the specific circumstances of the transaction, but the outcome may be less predictable compared to civil law systems.

13. Impact on International Arbitration

The differences between civil law and common law approaches also impact international arbitration. Arbitration proceedings may be influenced by the legal backgrounds of the arbitrators and the applicable law chosen by the parties. Understanding these differences is crucial for drafting arbitration clauses and preparing for arbitration in international sales disputes.

14. The Role of UNCITRAL and the CISG

The United Nations Commission on International Trade Law (UNCITRAL) and the United Nations Convention on Contracts for the International Sale of Goods (CISG) aim to harmonize international sales law by providing a uniform legal framework. The CISG combines elements of both civil law and common law, offering a balanced approach that can be applied globally. This harmonization effort helps to reduce legal barriers and facilitate cross-border trade.

15. Practical Considerations for Businesses

Businesses engaged in international sales must navigate the complexities of different legal systems. Understanding the distinctions between civil law and common law is essential for drafting effective contracts, managing risks, and resolving disputes. Companies should seek legal advice to ensure compliance with applicable laws and to leverage the benefits of both legal traditions.

16. Harmonization Efforts and Challenges

Efforts to harmonize international sales law face challenges due to the inherent differences between civil law and common law systems. While instruments like the CISG provide a common framework, the practical application of these rules can vary based on national legal traditions. Continued dialogue and collaboration among legal practitioners, scholars, and international organizations are necessary to address these challenges and promote greater harmonization.

17. Future Prospects for Harmonization

The future of international sales law will likely involve further efforts to harmonize legal principles and practices. Emerging technologies, such as blockchain and digital contracts, present new opportunities for standardization and innovation. Legal systems will need to adapt to these changes while maintaining the core principles of predictability, fairness, and efficiency in international trade.

18. Comparative Advantages and Disadvantages

Both civil law and common law systems have their advantages and disadvantages in the context of international sales. Civil law's codified approach provides clarity and predictability, while common law's flexibility allows for adaptation to specific circumstances. Understanding these comparative advantages can help businesses and legal practitioners choose the most appropriate legal framework for their international transactions.

19. Conclusion

The differences between civil law and common law approaches significantly impact the international sale of goods. While civil law systems offer structured and predictable rules, common law systems provide flexibility and adaptability. Harmonization efforts, such as the CISG, aim to bridge these differences and facilitate cross-border trade. By understanding the unique characteristics of both legal traditions, businesses can effectively navigate the complexities of international sales and mitigate legal risks.

20. Final Thoughts

In the ever-evolving landscape of international trade, legal practitioners must remain vigilant and adaptable. The interplay between civil law and common law will continue to shape the global marketplace, influencing contract drafting, dispute resolution, and legal compliance. By staying informed about the latest developments and trends, businesses and legal professionals can ensure that they are well-equipped to handle the challenges and opportunities of international commerce.

Impact on International Trade Practices:

1. Introduction to Legal Influences on Trade Practices

The differences between civil law and common law approaches significantly impact international trade practices. These legal systems shape how contracts are drafted, negotiated, and enforced, affecting the overall dynamics of international sales transactions. Understanding these differences is crucial for businesses to navigate the complexities of international trade effectively.

2. Contract Drafting: Emphasis on Formal Requirements vs. Flexibility

In civil law systems, contract drafting often emphasizes formal requirements and detailed provisions. Legal codes in civil law jurisdictions provide comprehensive rules that guide the formation and content of contracts. This results in contracts that are more structured and specific, reducing ambiguities and ensuring compliance with statutory requirements.

Conversely, common law systems prioritize the intentions and conduct of the parties involved. Contracts in common law jurisdictions may be less formal, with a greater focus on the commercial realities of the transaction. This flexibility allows for more adaptive and tailored contract terms, accommodating unique circumstances and business needs.

3. Negotiation Strategies: Structured Processes vs. Adaptive Approaches

The negotiation of international sales contracts is also influenced by the underlying legal system. In civil law countries, negotiations may follow more structured processes, with a strong emphasis on adhering to legal formalities and codified rules. Parties may rely on detailed contract templates that conform to statutory requirements.

In contrast, common law systems encourage a more adaptive approach to negotiations. Parties have greater freedom to negotiate terms based on their specific needs and preferences, without being constrained by rigid statutory requirements. This flexibility can lead to more innovative and customized contract solutions, fostering a collaborative negotiation environment.

4. Enforcement Mechanisms: Predictability vs. Judicial Discretion

The enforcement of international sales contracts varies significantly between civil law and common law systems. Civil law jurisdictions rely on codified rules and formal procedures to enforce contracts, providing a high degree of predictability and consistency. Courts in these jurisdictions apply statutory provisions strictly, reducing the scope for judicial discretion.

Common law systems, however, grant judges considerable discretion in interpreting and enforcing contracts. Courts may consider the broader context of the transaction, including prior dealings and trade practices, to determine the parties' intentions. While this approach offers flexibility, it can also result in less predictable outcomes, as judicial interpretations may vary.

5. Dispute Resolution: Formal Adjudication vs. Alternative Mechanisms

Dispute resolution practices differ markedly between civil law and common law systems. Civil law jurisdictions typically rely on formal adjudication processes, with courts applying codified rules to resolve disputes. This formal approach ensures that disputes are resolved in accordance with established legal principles, providing clarity and consistency.

In common law systems, alternative dispute resolution (ADR) mechanisms, such as arbitration and mediation, are more commonly used. These mechanisms offer flexible and efficient ways to resolve disputes outside of the formal court system. ADR can be particularly advantageous in international trade, as it allows parties to choose neutral forums and specialized arbitrators with expertise in commercial matters.

6. Risk Allocation: Codified Rules vs. Contractual Flexibility

Risk allocation in international sales contracts is influenced by the legal framework of the jurisdiction. Civil law systems provide detailed statutory provisions that allocate risks between the parties, such as rules on delivery, payment, and liability. These codified rules offer certainty but may limit the parties' ability to negotiate customized risk allocation terms.

Common law systems, on the other hand, emphasize contractual freedom, allowing parties to allocate risks based on their specific needs and preferences. This flexibility enables more precise risk management strategies, tailored to the unique circumstances of each transaction. However, it also requires careful drafting to ensure that risk allocation terms are clear and enforceable.

7. Case Study: Civil Law Influence on Contract Management

A German manufacturer enters into a contract with an Italian distributor for the sale of machinery. The contract is governed by German civil law, which requires detailed provisions on delivery, payment, and warranty. The parties rely on standardized contract templates that conform to statutory requirements, ensuring compliance with legal formalities. The structured nature of the contract minimizes ambiguities and provides a clear framework for managing the transaction.

8. Case Study: Common Law Influence on Contract Management

A British software company contracts with a Canadian buyer for the sale of customized software solutions. The contract is governed by English common law, which allows for more flexible and adaptive terms. The parties negotiate specific provisions on intellectual property rights, support services, and performance milestones, tailored to the unique requirements of the transaction. The flexibility of the common law system facilitates a collaborative negotiation process, resulting in a highly customized contract.

9. Legal Certainty and Business Confidence

Legal certainty is a critical factor in international trade practices. Civil law systems, with their detailed statutory provisions, provide a high degree of legal certainty, fostering business confidence. Companies operating in civil law jurisdictions can rely on clear and predictable rules, reducing the risk of legal disputes and enhancing the stability of their transactions.

In common law systems, legal certainty is achieved through the development of a rich body of case law. Judicial precedents provide guidance on the interpretation and application of legal principles, helping businesses anticipate potential outcomes. However, the reliance on judicial discretion can introduce variability, requiring companies to seek legal advice to navigate the complexities of common law.

10. Impact on Trade Logistics

The legal system also affects trade logistics, including the management of shipping, delivery, and transportation. Civil law jurisdictions often have detailed regulations governing logistics, ensuring that all aspects of the trade process are clearly defined. This can simplify logistics planning and execution, providing a structured framework for managing international shipments.

Common law jurisdictions, with their emphasis on contractual freedom, allow parties to negotiate logistics arrangements based on their specific needs. This flexibility can lead to more efficient and cost-effective logistics solutions, tailored to the unique requirements of each transaction. However, it also requires careful negotiation and drafting to ensure that logistics terms are clear and enforceable.

11. Case Study: Logistics in Civil Law Jurisdictions

A French exporter contracts with a Spanish importer for the sale of agricultural products. The contract, governed by French civil law, includes detailed provisions on delivery schedules, transportation methods, and quality standards. The structured nature of the contract ensures that all logistical aspects are clearly defined, reducing the risk of misunderstandings and delays. The parties rely on the statutory framework to manage the logistics of the transaction efficiently.

12. Case Study: Logistics in Common Law Jurisdictions

An Australian mining company contracts with a Japanese steel manufacturer for the supply of raw materials. The contract, governed by Australian common law, allows the parties to negotiate flexible logistics arrangements. They agree on specific delivery schedules, transportation methods, and quality control procedures, tailored to the unique requirements of the transaction. The flexibility of the common law system facilitates a collaborative logistics planning process, resulting in a more efficient and cost-effective solution.

13. Cross-Border Legal Compliance

Compliance with cross-border legal requirements is a critical aspect of international trade practices. Civil law systems provide detailed statutory guidelines that companies must follow, ensuring that all legal obligations are met. This structured approach can simplify compliance efforts, as companies have clear rules to adhere to.

In common law jurisdictions, compliance efforts may require a more nuanced understanding of both statutory requirements and judicial precedents. Companies must stay informed about legal developments and interpretive trends to ensure compliance with evolving legal standards. This dynamic approach can be challenging but also offers opportunities for more innovative compliance strategies.

14. Impact on Contractual Remedies

The availability and enforcement of contractual remedies are influenced by the legal system. Civil law jurisdictions provide a comprehensive set of statutory remedies, including specific performance, damages, and contract termination. These remedies are clearly defined and consistently applied, offering certainty for parties seeking to enforce their contractual rights.

Common law systems offer a broader range of remedies, with courts exercising discretion in awarding damages, specific performance, or other equitable relief. This flexibility allows for tailored solutions based on the specific circumstances of each case but can also introduce variability in outcomes. Understanding the available remedies and their enforcement is crucial for effective contract management.

15. Case Study: Remedies in Civil Law Jurisdictions

A Dutch supplier contracts with a Swiss buyer for the sale of industrial equipment. The contract is governed by Dutch civil law, which provides clear remedies for breach, including specific performance and damages. When the buyer fails to make payment, the supplier can rely on the statutory framework to seek enforcement of the contract through the courts. The availability of specific and predictable remedies ensures that the supplier's rights are protected.

16. Case Study: Remedies in Common Law Jurisdictions

A Canadian manufacturer contracts with an American retailer for the supply of consumer electronics. The contract is governed by U.S. common law, which offers a range of remedies for breach, including compensatory damages and specific performance. When the retailer fails to take delivery, the manufacturer can seek equitable relief through the courts. The flexibility of the common law system allows the court to tailor the remedy to the specific circumstances of the case, ensuring that justice is served.

17. Influence on Business Strategies

The legal system influences business strategies in international trade. Companies operating in civil law jurisdictions may adopt more conservative strategies, focusing on compliance with detailed statutory requirements. This approach can provide stability and reduce legal risks but may also limit flexibility and innovation.

In common law jurisdictions, companies may pursue more dynamic strategies, leveraging the flexibility of the legal system to negotiate customized contract terms and innovative solutions. This approach can enhance competitiveness and adaptability but may also require careful management of legal risks and uncertainties.

18. Legal Training and Expertise

Legal training and expertise are critical for navigating the complexities of international trade practices. Professionals in civil law jurisdictions must have a deep understanding of statutory provisions and their application, while those in common law jurisdictions must be adept at interpreting judicial precedents and case law. Cross-border transactions require legal practitioners to be proficient in both systems, ensuring that they can effectively advise clients and manage international sales contracts.

19. The Role of International Organizations

International organizations, such as the United Nations Commission on International Trade Law (UNCITRAL) and the International Chamber of Commerce (ICC), play a crucial role in bridging the gap between civil law and common law systems. These organizations develop harmonized legal instruments, such as the United Nations Convention on Contracts for the International Sale of Goods (CISG) and Incoterms, which provide a common framework for international sales. By promoting harmonization and standardization, these organizations help to reduce legal barriers and facilitate cross-border trade.

20. Conclusion: Harmonizing Legal Systems for Global Trade

The differences between civil law and common law approaches have a significant impact on international trade practices. While civil law systems provide structured and predictable rules, common law systems offer flexibility and adaptability. Understanding these differences is essential for businesses engaged in international trade, as it enables them to tailor their contract strategies to the specific legal environment and manage risks effectively. Continued efforts to harmonize and standardize international sales law, supported by international organizations, will be crucial for promoting global economic integration and facilitating cross-border trade.

TOPIC 10:

Issues and Challenges in the International Sale of Goods

Risk Allocation and Liability:

1. Importance of Risk Allocation in International Sales

Risk allocation is a fundamental aspect of international sales transactions, determining which party bears the risk of loss or damage to goods at various stages of the transaction. Proper risk allocation ensures that both the seller and buyer understand their responsibilities and can plan accordingly to mitigate potential losses. Clear risk allocation helps prevent disputes, facilitates smoother transactions, and provides a framework for liability management.

2. Role of Contract Types in Risk Allocation

Different contract types, such as FOB (Free on Board), CIF (Cost, Insurance, and Freight), and C&F (Cost and Freight), have distinct mechanisms for risk transfer. These mechanisms influence the point at which risk passes from the seller to the buyer, impacting the responsibilities of each party. Understanding these contract types and their implications is crucial for effectively managing risk in international sales transactions.

3. FOB Contracts and Risk Allocation

In FOB contracts, the seller's responsibility ends once the goods pass the ship's rail at the port of shipment. The buyer assumes all risks from that point onwards. This type of contract requires the buyer to manage transportation and insurance, making it suitable for buyers with logistical capabilities and expertise in international shipping. However, the buyer must be prepared to handle any risks or issues that arise during transit.

4. CIF Contracts and Risk Allocation

CIF contracts are more comprehensive, as the seller not only delivers the goods on board the vessel but also pays for the cost of transport to the destination port and obtains insurance for the goods during transit. The risk transfers to the buyer once the goods pass the ship's rail at the port of shipment. This arrangement provides added protection for the buyer and simplifies logistics, as the seller handles transportation and insurance.

5. C&F Contracts and Risk Allocation

C&F contracts are similar to CIF contracts but do not include insurance. The seller is responsible for delivering the goods on board the vessel and paying for the cost of transport to the destination port. The risk transfers to the buyer once the goods pass the ship's rail. Buyers must arrange their own insurance under C&F contracts, providing flexibility but also requiring careful management of potential risks during transit.

6. Legal Frameworks and Risk Allocation

The legal framework governing the transaction, including any applicable international conventions such as the CISG (United Nations Convention on Contracts for the International Sale of Goods), can significantly impact risk allocation and liability. The

CISG, for instance, provides standardized rules for international sales contracts, including provisions on risk transfer. Understanding these frameworks helps parties draft contracts that comply with international standards and reduce legal uncertainties.

7. Practical Considerations in Risk Allocation

When drafting contracts, parties must consider practical factors such as the nature of the goods, transportation methods, and the logistical capabilities of both the seller and buyer. For instance, perishable goods or high-value items may require more detailed risk allocation provisions to address specific issues that could arise during transit. Tailoring contract terms to the unique circumstances of the transaction ensures that risks are managed effectively.

8. Case Study: FOB Contract in Practice

Consider a case where a European electronics manufacturer enters into an FOB contract with an Asian distributor. The manufacturer delivers the goods on board the vessel at the port of shipment, transferring risk to the distributor. The distributor must manage transportation and insurance from that point onwards. This arrangement allows the manufacturer to focus on production and delivery while the distributor handles the complexities of international shipping.

9. Case Study: CIF Contract in Practice

In a CIF contract, a North American agricultural exporter agrees to deliver grain to a European buyer. The exporter arranges for transportation and insurance, ensuring that the goods are protected during transit. The risk transfers to the buyer once the goods pass the ship's rail. This comprehensive approach simplifies logistics for the buyer, who benefits from the added protection provided by the seller's insurance coverage.

10. Case Study: C&F Contract in Practice

A South American mining company enters into a C&F contract with an African steel manufacturer. The mining company delivers the ore on board the vessel and pays for transportation to the destination port. However, the buyer is responsible for arranging insurance. This arrangement allows the mining company to manage transportation logistics while giving the steel manufacturer the flexibility to choose their preferred insurance provider.

11. Drafting Contracts to Address Risk Allocation

Effective contract drafting requires a clear understanding of the chosen contract type and its implications for risk allocation. Parties must explicitly define the point at which risk transfers and outline the responsibilities of each party. Detailed clauses addressing transportation, insurance, and potential contingencies help prevent misunderstandings and disputes, ensuring that both parties are aware of their obligations.

12. The Role of Insurance in Risk Management

Insurance plays a crucial role in managing risks associated with international sales transactions. In CIF contracts, the seller's obligation to obtain insurance provides the buyer with added protection against potential losses. Even in C&F contracts, where the buyer arranges insurance, having appropriate coverage is essential for mitigating risks during transit. Understanding insurance requirements and ensuring adequate coverage is a key aspect of risk management.

13. Addressing Potential Disputes

Despite careful planning, disputes can arise in international sales transactions. Having clear contract terms and a well-defined risk allocation framework helps resolve disputes more effectively. Parties should also consider including dispute resolution mechanisms, such as arbitration or mediation clauses, to address potential issues. These mechanisms provide a structured process for resolving conflicts and ensuring that contractual obligations are upheld.

14. The Impact of Transportation Methods

The choice of transportation method, whether by sea, air, or land, can influence risk allocation and liability. Each method has its own risks and logistical considerations. For instance, maritime transport involves risks related to sea conditions and potential delays, while air transport may involve higher costs but faster delivery times. Understanding these factors helps parties tailor their risk management strategies accordingly.

15. Regulatory Compliance and Risk Management

Compliance with international and domestic regulations is essential for managing risks in international sales transactions. Parties must be aware of customs requirements, import/export controls, and other regulatory obligations. Non-compliance can result in delays, penalties, and increased risks. Ensuring that contracts address regulatory compliance helps mitigate these risks and ensures smooth transaction execution.

16. The Role of Technology in Risk Management

Technological advancements, such as blockchain and digital tracking systems, offer new ways to manage risks in international sales transactions. These technologies provide greater transparency and traceability, allowing parties to monitor the movement of goods in real-time and address potential issues promptly. Integrating technology into risk management strategies can enhance efficiency and reduce the likelihood of disputes.

17. The Interplay of Legal Systems

In cross-border transactions, the interplay between different legal systems can impact risk allocation and liability. Understanding the legal principles and practices of the jurisdictions involved helps parties navigate potential conflicts and ensure that their contracts are enforceable. Harmonizing contract terms with applicable legal standards and seeking legal advice when necessary are essential steps in managing cross-border risks.

18. The Importance of Clear Communication

Clear and effective communication between the seller and buyer is crucial for managing risks and ensuring that both parties understand their responsibilities. Regular updates on the status of the goods, potential issues, and compliance with contract terms help maintain transparency and trust. Establishing open communication channels and documenting all relevant information can prevent misunderstandings and facilitate timely resolution of any problems.

19. Mitigating Risks Through Contingency Planning

Contingency planning is an important aspect of risk management in international sales transactions. Parties should anticipate potential issues, such as delays, damage to goods, or regulatory changes, and outline contingency measures in the contract. Having a well-defined plan for addressing unforeseen circumstances helps ensure that the transaction can proceed smoothly and that risks are effectively managed.

20. Conclusion: Effective Risk Management in International Sales

Risk allocation and liability are critical components of international sales transactions. By understanding the mechanisms provided by different contract types, considering practical and legal factors, and drafting clear and comprehensive contracts, parties can effectively manage risks and liabilities. Incorporating insurance, addressing potential disputes, and leveraging technology further enhance risk management strategies. Through careful planning and clear communication, businesses can navigate the complexities of international sales and ensure successful and secure transactions.

Encyclopedia   - **THE PATRON** -   .224

TOPIC 11:

Dispute Resolution Mechanisms

Marwan M. Alarjan   - **MASTR** -   Martin Apollo Bureau

Importance of Dispute Resolution Mechanisms:

Dispute resolution mechanisms are essential in international sales transactions due to the complexity and potential for conflicts that arise in cross-border trade. These mechanisms provide structured ways to address and resolve disputes, ensuring that business relationships can be maintained and legal uncertainties minimized. Selecting the appropriate dispute resolution method and clearly outlining these provisions in the contract are crucial for efficient and effective conflict management.

Arbitration as a Preferred Mechanism

Arbitration is often favored in international sales disputes due to its flexibility and confidentiality. Unlike litigation, arbitration allows parties to select arbitrators with specific expertise, ensuring a more informed decision-making process. Additionally, arbitration proceedings are private, protecting sensitive commercial information from public disclosure. The enforceability of arbitration awards under the New York

Convention, which has been adopted by over 160 countries, further enhances its attractiveness, providing a reliable means of resolving disputes with international enforceability.

Benefits and Drawbacks of Arbitration

While arbitration offers many advantages, it also has its drawbacks. The cost of arbitration can be high, particularly in complex cases that require multiple arbitrators and extensive legal representation. Additionally, the lack of formal discovery procedures in some arbitration systems can be a disadvantage, limiting the parties' ability to gather evidence. Despite these challenges, the ability to enforce arbitration awards globally and the flexibility it offers often outweigh the disadvantages for many businesses.

Mediation: A Collaborative Approach

Mediation presents a collaborative approach to dispute resolution, focusing on mutual agreement rather than adjudication. It allows parties to maintain control over the outcome and fosters a cooperative atmosphere that can preserve business relationships. Mediation can be faster and less costly than arbitration or litigation, making it an attractive option for resolving disputes amicably. However, mediation relies heavily on the willingness of both parties to negotiate in good faith, and there is no guarantee of reaching a resolution.

The Role of Litigation in International Disputes

Litigation provides a formal and structured legal framework for resolving disputes, offering clear procedural rules and the ability to appeal decisions. Courts have the authority to compel disclosure of evidence, which can be critical in complex cases. However, litigation can be time-consuming, expensive, and public, potentially damaging business reputations and relationships. Jurisdictional issues and the enforcement of foreign judgments can further complicate international litigation.

Enforcement of Arbitration Awards

The New York Convention on the Recognition and Enforcement of Foreign Arbitral Awards is a key instrument in ensuring the enforceability of arbitration awards across borders. By requiring member states to recognize and enforce arbitration awards, the Convention provides a significant advantage for arbitration over litigation. However, enforcement can still face challenges, such as the refusal of enforcement based on public policy grounds or procedural irregularities.

Enforcement of Court Judgments

Enforcing foreign court judgments can be more complex than enforcing arbitration awards. It often depends on bilateral or multilateral treaties and the specific laws of the enforcing jurisdiction. The lack of a universal convention equivalent to the New York Convention for court judgments means that parties may face significant hurdles in securing enforcement. Understanding the legal landscape and including enforceable dispute resolution provisions in contracts is crucial for managing this risk.

Case Study: Arbitration in Practice

Consider a scenario where a European electronics company and an Asian supplier have a dispute over the quality of goods delivered. Opting for arbitration under the ICC (International Chamber of Commerce) rules, they select arbitrators with specific expertise in electronics and international trade. The arbitration process, conducted privately and efficiently, results in an award in favor of the European company. Due to the New York Convention, this award is enforceable in the supplier's home country, providing a predictable and secure resolution to the dispute.

Case Study: Mediation in Practice

In another example, a North American agricultural exporter and a European importer face a disagreement over delivery terms. They choose mediation to resolve their differences, engaging a neutral mediator with experience in international trade. Through a series of mediated sessions, they reach a mutually acceptable settlement, preserving their business relationship and avoiding the costs and time associated with arbitration or litigation.

Drafting Effective Dispute Resolution Clauses

Drafting clear and effective dispute resolution clauses is vital for ensuring that disputes are resolved efficiently. These clauses should specify the chosen method (arbitration, mediation, or litigation), the governing rules (such as ICC or UNCITRAL for arbitration), the seat of arbitration or jurisdiction for litigation, and the language of proceedings. Including detailed provisions can help prevent ambiguities and ensure that both parties understand their rights and obligations.

Choosing the Appropriate Dispute Resolution Mechanism

The choice of dispute resolution mechanism should be based on the specific needs and preferences of the parties involved. Factors to consider include the nature of the transaction, the relationship between the parties, the need for confidentiality, the legal systems involved, and the potential costs and duration of the process. By carefully considering these factors, parties can select the mechanism that best suits their situation.

The Role of Legal Advisors

Legal advisors play a crucial role in guiding businesses through the complexities of international dispute resolution. Their expertise in drafting dispute resolution clauses, understanding the legal implications of different mechanisms, and navigating the enforcement process is invaluable. Engaging experienced legal counsel can help businesses avoid common pitfalls and ensure that their interests are protected.

International Institutions and Dispute Resolution

International institutions such as the ICC, the London Court of International Arbitration (LCIA), and the American Arbitration Association (AAA) provide established frameworks and rules for arbitration and mediation. These institutions offer administrative support, ensure the neutrality of arbitrators or mediators, and uphold the integrity of the process. Their involvement can enhance the credibility and enforceability of the dispute resolution process.

Impact of Technological Advances

Technological advances, such as virtual hearings and online dispute resolution (ODR), are transforming the landscape of international dispute resolution. These technologies offer greater accessibility, reduce costs, and increase efficiency. Virtual hearings, for example, enable parties to participate from different locations, making the process more flexible and accommodating. ODR platforms provide a digital environment for resolving disputes, streamlining communication and documentation.

Challenges and Criticisms of Arbitration

Despite its advantages, arbitration is not without its critics. Concerns include the high costs associated with complex cases, the potential for arbitrator bias, and the limited scope for appealing arbitration awards. Addressing these criticisms requires ongoing efforts to enhance transparency, reduce costs, and ensure the impartiality and competence of arbitrators.

Challenges and Criticisms of Mediation

Mediation's reliance on voluntary participation and mutual agreement can be both a strength and a weakness. While it promotes collaboration and preserves relationships, it may not be effective if one party is unwilling to negotiate in good faith. Additionally, the lack of a binding resolution can lead to prolonged disputes if mediation fails. To mitigate these challenges, parties can consider hybrid approaches, such as med-arb, which combine mediation and arbitration.

Future Trends in Dispute Resolution

The future of dispute resolution in international sales transactions is likely to be shaped by continued technological advancements, greater emphasis on sustainability and ethical practices, and evolving legal frameworks. The integration of artificial intelligence (AI) in dispute resolution, for instance, could enhance the efficiency and accuracy of decision-making processes. Additionally, the growing focus on corporate social responsibility (CSR) may influence the choice of dispute resolution mechanisms, with parties seeking methods that align with their ethical values.

Conclusion: The Evolving Landscape of Dispute Resolution

Dispute resolution mechanisms are critical for managing conflicts in international sales transactions. Arbitration, mediation, and litigation each offer distinct advantages and challenges, and the choice of mechanism should be tailored to the specific needs of the parties involved. By understanding the legal and practical considerations, drafting effective dispute resolution clauses, and leveraging the expertise of legal advisors and international institutions, businesses can navigate disputes efficiently and effectively. As the landscape of international trade continues to evolve, staying abreast of emerging trends and technologies will be essential for ensuring the continued effectiveness of dispute resolution mechanisms.

TOPIC 12:

Impact of Digitalization and E-Commerce

Legal Challenges in Electronic Contracting and Digital Signatures

The digitalization of trade and the rise of e-commerce have revolutionized the international sale of goods, presenting both opportunities and challenges. One of the primary challenges is ensuring the validity and security of electronic contracts and digital signatures. Traditional legal principles governing contract formation and enforcement need to be adapted to accommodate electronic transactions. This includes recognizing the legal validity of digital signatures and ensuring that electronic contracts meet the necessary requirements for enforceability. The adoption of international frameworks, such as the UNCITRAL Model Law on Electronic Commerce and the UN Convention on the Use of Electronic Communications in International Contracts, has been instrumental in addressing these issues. However, differences in national laws and varying levels of technological infrastructure can still pose significant challenges.

Data Protection and Privacy Concerns

Another critical issue arising from the digitalization of trade is data protection and privacy. The increasing use of e-commerce platforms involves the collection and processing of vast amounts of personal data. Ensuring compliance with data protection regulations, such as the General Data Protection Regulation (GDPR) in the European Union, is essential for businesses engaged in international sales. These regulations impose stringent requirements on data collection, storage, and transfer, aiming to protect consumers' privacy and personal information. Businesses must navigate the complexities of cross-border data flows and implement robust data protection measures to prevent breaches and ensure compliance. Failure to do so can result in severe legal and reputational consequences.

Adapting Traditional Legal Principles

The growth of e-commerce platforms and digital marketplaces necessitates a re-evaluation of traditional legal principles to accommodate the unique characteristics of digital trade. For instance, the principles of jurisdiction and applicable law, which determine the legal framework governing a transaction, become more complex in the context of online sales. E-commerce platforms often operate across multiple jurisdictions, leading to potential conflicts of laws. Furthermore, issues related to consumer protection, intellectual property rights, and cybersecurity require a modernized approach to legal regulation. Developing legal strategies that address these evolving challenges is crucial for ensuring the smooth functioning of digital trade and protecting the interests of all stakeholders.

Leveraging Opportunities in the Digital Economy

Despite these challenges, the digitalization of trade offers significant opportunities for businesses to expand their reach and enhance operational efficiency. E-commerce platforms enable businesses to access global markets, reducing barriers to entry and increasing competition. Digital tools and technologies, such as blockchain and artificial intelligence, can improve supply chain transparency, reduce transaction costs, and enhance trust between trading partners. To fully leverage these opportunities, businesses must stay abreast of technological advancements and adapt their legal and operational strategies accordingly. This includes investing in digital infrastructure, adopting best practices in cybersecurity, and ensuring compliance with international legal standards. By doing so, businesses can thrive in the digital economy and capitalize on the benefits of digitalization and e-commerce.

In conclusion, the impact of digitalization and e-commerce on the international sale of goods is profound, requiring a comprehensive understanding of the legal challenges and opportunities it presents. Ensuring the validity and security of electronic contracts, addressing data protection concerns, adapting traditional legal principles, and leveraging new technological opportunities are all essential for navigating the evolving landscape of digital trade. By proactively addressing these issues, businesses can successfully engage in international sales and harness the full potential of the digital economy.

Future Trends and Emerging Issues

The international sale of goods is continuously evolving, with new trends and emerging issues shaping the landscape of global trade. These trends include the increasing importance of sustainability and environmental considerations, the impact of geopolitical developments, and the growth of regional trade agreements. Understanding these trends and their implications for international sales is essential for businesses and legal practitioners to stay ahead of the curve and navigate the complexities of the global market.

Sustainability and environmental considerations are becoming increasingly important in international trade, with consumers and regulators demanding more sustainable practices. This trend is influencing contract terms, supply chain management, and corporate responsibility initiatives. Geopolitical developments, such as trade wars and shifting alliances, can also impact international sales by creating uncertainties and altering trade patterns. Additionally, the growth of regional trade agreements, such as the Comprehensive and Progressive Agreement for Trans-Pacific Partnership (CPTPP), is shaping the legal framework for international sales by promoting greater harmonization and cooperation among member countries.

By understanding these future trends and emerging issues, businesses and legal practitioners can develop strategies that address the evolving challenges and opportunities of the international sale of goods. This proactive approach can help ensure that international sales transactions are conducted efficiently, sustainably, and in compliance with applicable legal standards.

Conclusion

The international sale of goods, a cornerstone of global commerce, presents a myriad of complexities and challenges that require a deep understanding of various principles, legal frameworks, and contract types. As we have explored, the intricacies of contract formation, risk allocation, dispute resolution, and the impact of digitalization and e-commerce are crucial for businesses and legal practitioners engaged in international trade. By comprehensively analyzing these aspects, stakeholders can better navigate the legal landscape, ensuring that transactions are conducted smoothly and efficiently.

One of the key takeaways from this assessment is the importance of understanding and correctly applying different contract types such as FOB, CIF, C&F, and FAS. Each contract type offers distinct advantages and poses specific challenges, especially in terms of risk allocation and cost responsibilities. By selecting the appropriate contract type and clearly defining the obligations of each party, businesses can minimize disputes and ensure that their international sales transactions are legally sound and commercially viable. Furthermore, the rise of digitalization and e-commerce necessitates a re-evaluation of traditional legal principles to accommodate the unique characteristics of online trade. Addressing issues such as electronic contracting, digital signatures, and data protection is vital for maintaining the validity and security of digital transactions.

Additionally, the harmonization of international sales law through instruments like the CISG plays a pivotal role in reducing legal uncertainties and facilitating cross-border trade. However, challenges remain, including the need for greater awareness and consistent application of the CISG, as well as the interplay between the CISG and domestic laws. Continuous education and harmonization efforts are essential to ensure that the CISG remains effective in promoting a uniform legal framework for international sales.

Looking forward, it is clear that the international sale of goods will continue to evolve in response to emerging trends and technological advancements. Stakeholders must remain vigilant and adaptable, embracing continuous learning and collaboration to stay ahead of these changes. By doing so, businesses and legal practitioners can not only mitigate risks but also capitalize on new opportunities, driving economic growth, innovation, and cultural exchange on a global scale. Through a collective effort to enhance understanding, improve legal frameworks, and address emerging challenges, the international sale of goods will remain a vital and dynamic component of international commercial law, fostering a more interconnected and prosperous global economy.

CHAPTER II
CARRIAGE OF GOODS BY SEA

Overview of Maritime Law

Maritime law, also known as admiralty law, is a specialized field that governs maritime questions and offenses, blending both domestic and international regulations to address a variety of issues related to shipping, navigation, waters, commerce, and marine resources. Given that over 90% of the world's trade is conducted by sea, maritime law plays a pivotal role in facilitating and regulating international trade. Its significance extends to various areas, including the carriage of goods, marine insurance, ship ownership and registration, maritime liens, and the rights and responsibilities of shipmasters, crew, and passengers.

Maritime law's unique principles and frameworks are tailored to address the specificities of maritime activities. These principles, which have evolved over centuries, are deeply rooted in historical traditions and have been adapted to meet contemporary legal practices. The primary aim of maritime law is to balance the promotion of free trade with the protection of the interests of all parties involved in maritime commerce, ensuring that the seas remain safe and navigable for commercial activities.

One of the fundamental aspects of maritime law is the regulation of shipping. This includes the rules governing the registration of ships, the documentation required for vessels, and the legal requirements for operating ships. Ship registration is crucial as it determines the nationality of the vessel and the legal jurisdiction under which it operates. Maritime law also stipulates the qualifications and responsibilities of shipmasters and crew, ensuring that those in charge of operating vessels are adequately trained and capable of ensuring the safety and security of the vessel, its cargo, and its passengers.

Another critical component of maritime law is the carriage of goods by sea. This involves the legal frameworks governing the transportation of goods over water, including the rights and obligations of carriers and shippers. Key conventions such as the Hague-Visby Rules, the Hamburg Rules, and the Rotterdam Rules provide standardized regulations that aim to harmonize the rules for the carriage of goods by sea, thereby facilitating international trade by reducing legal uncertainties and disputes.

Marine insurance is another pivotal area regulated by maritime law. Marine insurance provides financial protection against the risks associated with maritime activities, including the loss or damage of ships and cargo, as well as liabilities arising from maritime accidents. Maritime law governs the terms and conditions of marine insurance policies, the responsibilities of insurers and insured parties, and the procedures for claiming and settling insurance disputes. This ensures that the financial risks associated with maritime trade are managed effectively, promoting stability and confidence in the maritime industry.

Maritime liens and mortgages are also essential elements of maritime law. These legal mechanisms provide security interests in ships and cargo, allowing creditors to claim against these assets in the event of non-payment or default. Maritime liens arise from various sources, including unpaid wages of crew members, salvage operations, and claims for damage caused by the ship. Maritime law provides specific procedures for enforcing these liens, ensuring that the rights of creditors are protected while maintaining the smooth operation of maritime commerce.

The enforcement of maritime claims and the resolution of maritime disputes are crucial aspects of maritime law. This includes the jurisdiction of admiralty courts, the procedures for arresting and detaining ships, and the methods for resolving disputes through arbitration or litigation. Admiralty courts have specialized knowledge and expertise in handling maritime cases, providing a forum for the fair and efficient resolution of disputes. Maritime arbitration is also widely used as an alternative dispute resolution mechanism, offering a flexible and confidential process for resolving maritime disputes.

International conventions and treaties play a significant role in harmonizing maritime law across different jurisdictions. Conventions such as the United Nations Convention on the Law of the Sea (UNCLOS) establish comprehensive frameworks for the regulation of maritime activities, including the rights and responsibilities of states in relation to maritime zones, navigation, and the exploitation of marine resources. These conventions promote international cooperation and ensure that maritime law is applied consistently and fairly across different countries, facilitating global trade and commerce.

The regulation of marine pollution and environmental protection is another vital area of maritime law. Conventions such as the International Convention for the Prevention of Pollution from Ships (MARPOL) set out rules and standards for preventing pollution from ships, protecting the marine environment from the harmful effects of maritime activities. Maritime law also includes provisions for responding to marine pollution incidents, including the responsibilities of shipowners, operators, and states in preventing and mitigating the impact of such incidents.

The protection of seafarers' rights is an important aspect of maritime law. International conventions such as the Maritime Labour Convention (MLC) set out minimum standards for the working and living conditions of seafarers, including provisions for employment contracts, wages, hours of work and rest, and health and safety. Maritime law ensures that seafarers are treated fairly and with respect, recognizing the essential role they play in the global maritime industry.

In recent years, maritime law has had to adapt to new challenges and developments in the maritime industry. This includes the regulation of emerging technologies such as autonomous ships and the use of digital platforms for maritime trade. Maritime law must evolve to address the legal and regulatory implications of these innovations, ensuring that they are integrated into the maritime industry in a way that promotes safety, security, and efficiency.

The global nature of maritime trade means that maritime law must be dynamic and responsive to the changing needs of the industry. This requires continuous collaboration and cooperation between international organizations, national governments, and industry stakeholders to develop and implement effective legal frameworks. By doing so, maritime law can continue to support the growth and development of the global maritime industry, ensuring that it remains a vital component of the world's economy.

One practical implication of the complex nature of maritime law is the need for specialized legal expertise. Legal practitioners in the field of maritime law must have a deep understanding of both international conventions and national regulations, as well as the specific practices and customs of the maritime industry. This expertise is essential for advising clients on a wide range of issues, from drafting and negotiating contracts to resolving disputes and navigating the regulatory landscape.

In conclusion, maritime law is a multifaceted and dynamic field that plays a crucial role in regulating and facilitating international maritime trade. Its principles and frameworks are designed to address the unique challenges and complexities of maritime activities, ensuring that the seas remain safe, secure, and accessible for commercial purposes. Through continuous evolution and adaptation, maritime law will continue to support the growth and development of the global maritime industry, promoting economic prosperity and international cooperation. To further delve into the intricacies of maritime law, consider the following question:

How can maritime law evolve to address the emerging challenges posed by technological advancements, such as autonomous vessels, while ensuring the protection of maritime stakeholders' rights and the preservation of environmental standards?

Historical Evolution and Sources of Maritime Law

The origins of maritime law can be traced back to ancient civilizations such as the Phoenicians, Greeks, and Romans, who established early maritime codes to govern sea trade. The medieval period saw the development of the "Law of the Sea," with notable contributions from the Rhodian Sea Law and the Laws of Oleron, which provided foundational principles for modern maritime law. The evolution of maritime law continued through the Renaissance and the Enlightenment, with the adoption of various international treaties and conventions that standardized maritime practices across different jurisdictions.

The primary sources of maritime law include international conventions, treaties, domestic legislation, and customary law. Key international conventions that have significantly influenced maritime law include the International Convention for the Safety of Life at Sea (SOLAS), the International Convention on Load Lines, the International Convention for the Prevention of Pollution from Ships (MARPOL), and the United Nations Convention on the Law of the Sea (UNCLOS). These conventions provide a framework for regulating various aspects of maritime activities, ensuring uniformity and consistency in maritime law across different countries.

Key Principles of Maritime Law

Maritime law is built on several key principles that govern maritime activities and ensure the orderly conduct of maritime commerce. One of the fundamental principles is the concept of "freedom of the seas," which promotes the free and unrestricted use of the world's oceans for navigation and trade. This principle is enshrined in UNCLOS, which establishes the legal framework for maritime activities and delineates the rights and responsibilities of coastal and landlocked states.

Another critical principle is the "right of innocent passage," which allows ships of all nations to navigate through territorial waters of other states without hindrance, provided they do not threaten the peace, security, or order of the coastal state. This principle facilitates international trade by ensuring that ships can transit through key maritime routes without undue interference.

Carriage of Goods and Marine Insurance

The carriage of goods by sea is a central aspect of maritime law, governed by various international conventions such as the Hague-Visby Rules, the Hamburg Rules, and the Rotterdam Rules. These conventions establish the rights and obligations of carriers and shippers, including provisions related to the issuance of bills of lading, the liability of carriers for loss or damage to goods, and the limitation of liability.

Marine insurance is another crucial component of maritime law, providing financial protection against risks associated with maritime activities. Marine insurance policies cover a wide range of perils, including damage to ships and cargo, piracy, and natural disasters. The principles of marine insurance are codified in international conventions and domestic legislation, ensuring uniformity in the application of insurance law across different jurisdictions.

Ship Ownership and Registration

The ownership and registration of ships are governed by both international conventions and national laws. The process of ship registration involves the documentation of a vessel's ownership and its compliance with safety and environmental standards. Registered ships are granted nationality and are entitled to fly the flag of the registering state, which provides protection and oversight in international waters.

Maritime law also addresses issues related to ship mortgages and liens, which are critical for securing financing for shipbuilding and maintenance. Maritime liens provide creditors with a legal claim against a vessel for unpaid debts, ensuring that the interests of lenders and other stakeholders are protected.

Maritime Liens and Claims

Maritime liens and claims are unique aspects of maritime law, providing security interests in vessels for the satisfaction of maritime debts. These liens arise from various maritime transactions, such as salvage operations, crew wages, and damage caused by the vessel. Maritime liens have priority over other claims and can be enforced through the arrest and sale of the vessel.

The enforcement of maritime claims involves complex legal procedures, including the arrest of ships, judicial sales, and the distribution of proceeds among claimants. These procedures are governed by international conventions and national laws, ensuring that maritime claims are resolved fairly and efficiently.

Rights and Responsibilities of Shipmasters, Crew, and Passengers

Maritime law outlines the rights and responsibilities of shipmasters, crew, and passengers, ensuring the safe and efficient operation of vessels. Shipmasters are responsible for the overall command and navigation of the vessel, including compliance with safety and environmental regulations. Crew members have specific duties related to the operation and maintenance of the vessel, and their rights are protected under international conventions such as the Maritime Labour Convention (MLC).

Passengers on board ships are also protected by maritime law, which sets out provisions related to their safety, health, and welfare. International conventions such as the Athens Convention establish the liability of carriers for passenger injuries and losses, ensuring that passengers have legal recourse in the event of accidents or incidents at sea.

Challenges and Future Directions in Maritime Law

Despite its comprehensive framework, maritime law faces several challenges in addressing contemporary issues such as piracy, maritime terrorism, and environmental protection. The rise of cyber threats and technological advancements in shipping also present new legal challenges, requiring continuous adaptation of maritime law to keep pace with these developments.

Environmental protection has become a significant focus in maritime law, with increasing emphasis on reducing pollution from ships and promoting sustainable maritime practices. International conventions such as MARPOL and the Ballast Water Management Convention aim to mitigate the environmental impact of shipping activities, ensuring the preservation of marine ecosystems.

Conclusion

Maritime law is a complex and dynamic field that plays a critical role in regulating international trade and ensuring the safe and efficient operation of maritime activities. Its principles and frameworks are designed to address the specificities of maritime commerce, balancing the promotion of free trade with the protection of the interests of all parties involved. As maritime activities continue to evolve, maritime law must adapt to address new challenges and opportunities, ensuring the continued stability and predictability of the global maritime industry. Through continuous collaboration and harmonization of international conventions and national laws, maritime law can effectively support the growth and development of global trade.

Encyclopedia   - **THE PATRON** -   .260

TOPIC 1:

International Conventions

Marwan M. Alarjan   - **MASTR** -   Martin Apollo Bureau

Role and Importance of International Conventions

International conventions are essential in harmonizing maritime laws across different jurisdictions. They establish standardized regulations and procedures that facilitate smooth and predictable international maritime trade. By providing a uniform legal framework, these conventions reduce the complexities and uncertainties associated with cross-border maritime activities, thereby promoting global trade efficiency and cooperation.

The Hague-Visby Rules: Overview and Impact

The Hague-Visby Rules, an amendment to the original Hague Rules, are one of the most widely adopted international conventions in maritime law. They govern the carriage of goods by sea, establishing the rights and obligations of carriers and shippers. The Hague-Visby Rules provide a balanced framework that addresses issues such as liability for loss or damage to cargo, the issuance of bills of lading, and the limitation of liability for carriers. Their adoption by numerous countries has significantly contributed to the standardization of maritime law, reducing legal disputes and enhancing trade predictability.

Criticisms of the Hague-Visby Rules

Despite their widespread acceptance, the Hague-Visby Rules have faced criticism for being outdated and not adequately addressing modern shipping practices. Critics argue that the rules fail to consider advancements in shipping technology and changes in global trade dynamics. Furthermore, the limitation of liability provisions is seen by some as disproportionately favoring carriers over shippers, potentially leading to unfair outcomes in certain cases.

The Hamburg Rules: A More Shipper-Friendly Approach

In response to the perceived limitations of the Hague-Visby Rules, the Hamburg Rules were developed under the auspices of the United Nations in 1978. The Hamburg Rules aim to provide a more balanced approach, offering greater protection to shippers and reflecting contemporary shipping practices. They address issues such as the carrier's liability for delay in delivery and extend the scope of the carrier's responsibility. However, the Hamburg Rules have not been as widely adopted as the Hague-Visby Rules, limiting their global impact.

The Rotterdam Rules: Modernizing Maritime Law

The Rotterdam Rules, adopted in 2008, represent a comprehensive effort to modernize maritime law and address the shortcomings of previous conventions. These rules cover a broader scope of transportation, including multimodal transport involving sea legs. The Rotterdam Rules introduce more detailed provisions on electronic documentation, liability regimes, and the obligations of all parties involved in the shipping process. They aim to provide a more cohesive and updated framework that aligns with current shipping and trade practices.

Challenges in Implementing the Rotterdam Rules

While the Rotterdam Rules offer a modernized approach to maritime law, their implementation has faced challenges. The rules have not yet achieved the widespread ratification needed to replace older conventions like the Hague-Visby Rules. This lack of adoption can be attributed to various factors, including resistance from countries with established legal systems based on the older conventions and the complexity of transitioning to a new legal framework.

Harmonization vs. Regional Specificities

One of the critical issues in the adoption of international conventions is the tension between harmonization and regional specificities. While harmonized rules provide uniformity and predictability, they may not account for the unique legal, economic, and operational conditions of different regions. This can lead to challenges in implementation and enforcement, as countries may need to adapt international standards to fit their domestic contexts.

The Role of International Bodies in Promoting Conventions

International bodies such as the International Maritime Organization (IMO) and the United Nations Commission on International Trade Law (UNCITRAL) play a crucial role in promoting the adoption and implementation of international conventions. These organizations facilitate dialogue among member states, provide technical assistance, and develop guidelines to support the harmonization of maritime laws. Their efforts are essential in overcoming the challenges associated with the adoption of new conventions.

Case Studies: Impact of International Conventions

Examining case studies can provide valuable insights into the impact of international conventions on maritime trade. For example, the implementation of the Hague-Visby Rules has been shown to reduce legal disputes and enhance the efficiency of maritime transactions in countries that have adopted them. Similarly, the Rotterdam Rules have the potential to streamline multimodal transport operations, although their full impact remains to be seen due to limited adoption.

Future Directions and Prospects

The future of international conventions in maritime law will likely involve continued efforts to balance harmonization with regional specificities. As global trade evolves, there will be a need for ongoing updates to existing conventions and the development of new frameworks that address emerging challenges, such as cybersecurity threats and environmental sustainability. The success of these efforts will depend on the willingness of countries to collaborate and adapt their legal systems to align with international standards, ensuring the smooth and predictable operation of global maritime trade.

Hague-Visby Rules :

Historical Context and Adoption

The Hague-Visby Rules, originating from the Hague Rules of 1924 and amended by the Visby Protocol in 1968, were developed to standardize international shipping laws and provide a uniform framework for the carriage of goods by sea. The aim was to balance the interests of carriers and shippers, reducing disputes and providing clear guidelines on carrier liability. The adoption of these rules was a significant step towards harmonizing maritime law, which was previously fragmented by varying national regulations.

Key Provisions and Scope

The Hague-Visby Rules outline the rights and responsibilities of carriers and shippers under a bill of lading. They establish the carrier's liability for loss or damage to goods from the time they are loaded onto the ship until they are discharged. The rules specify the carrier's duty to exercise due diligence to make the ship seaworthy, properly man, equip, and supply the vessel, and ensure that the holds are fit and safe for cargo. These provisions aim to ensure the safe and efficient transportation of goods, protecting the interests of shippers.

Liability Limits and Defenses

One of the critical features of the Hague-Visby Rules is the limitation of liability for carriers. The rules set a monetary limit per package or unit of goods, which was a significant change introduced by the Visby Protocol to address inflation and changing economic conditions. This limitation protects carriers from excessive financial burdens in case of loss or damage but has been a point of contention for shippers who may find the compensation insufficient. The rules also provide carriers with specific defenses against liability, such as acts of God, war, and inherent defects in the goods.

Impact on International Trade

The Hague-Visby Rules have had a profound impact on international trade by providing a predictable legal framework that facilitates the smooth operation of global maritime commerce. By establishing clear liability rules, the Hague-Visby Rules reduce the risk of disputes and litigation, thus lowering transaction costs and fostering a more stable trading environment. This predictability is crucial for international trade, where parties often operate under different legal systems and need a common set of rules to govern their transactions.

Criticisms and Limitations

Despite their widespread adoption, the Hague-Visby Rules have faced criticism for being outdated and not adequately reflecting modern shipping practices and technologies. Critics argue that the liability limits are too low to provide adequate compensation for high-value goods. Additionally, the rules are seen as overly favorable to carriers, providing numerous defenses that can limit their liability. These criticisms highlight the need for ongoing reforms to adapt the legal framework to contemporary needs.

Comparison with Other Conventions

Comparing the Hague-Visby Rules with other maritime conventions, such as the Hamburg Rules and the Rotterdam Rules, reveals different approaches to carrier liability and shipper protection. The Hamburg Rules, for instance, are considered more shipper-friendly, imposing stricter liability on carriers and higher compensation limits. The Rotterdam Rules aim to modernize and expand the scope of maritime law to include multimodal transport, addressing some of the limitations of the Hague-Visby Rules. However, the Rotterdam Rules have not yet achieved widespread adoption, leaving the Hague-Visby Rules as the prevailing standard.

Case Law and Interpretation

Judicial interpretation and case law play a vital role in the application of the Hague-Visby Rules. Courts in different jurisdictions have developed a body of case law that clarifies ambiguous terms and addresses specific issues arising under the rules. This case law contributes to the uniform application of the rules but can also lead to divergent interpretations, depending on the jurisdiction. Understanding the key judicial decisions and trends is essential for navigating the complexities of the Hague-Visby Rules.

Practical Challenges

Implementing the Hague-Visby Rules can present practical challenges for carriers and shippers. For example, determining the package or unit for liability purposes can be contentious, particularly when goods are shipped in containers with multiple items. Additionally, proving due diligence and seaworthiness can be complex and fact-intensive, requiring thorough documentation and evidence. These practical challenges underscore the importance of clear contractual terms and effective risk management strategies.

Relevance in Modern Shipping

The relevance of the Hague-Visby Rules in modern shipping continues to be debated. While the rules provide a well-established framework that many countries rely on, they may not fully address the realities of contemporary maritime trade, such as the rise of containerization, digital documentation, and increased cargo values. Ongoing discussions about updating or replacing the rules with more comprehensive frameworks, like the Rotterdam Rules, reflect the need for continuous evolution in maritime law.

Future Prospects

Looking ahead, the future of the Hague-Visby Rules will likely involve balancing the need for stability and predictability with the demand for modernization and reform. Enhancing the rules to better protect shippers, increase liability limits, and accommodate technological advancements could make them more relevant and effective. Continued international collaboration and dialogue among stakeholders will be essential to ensure that maritime law evolves in line with the changing landscape of global trade, ultimately benefiting all parties involved in maritime commerce.

Hamburg Rules :

Introduction and Historical Context

The Hamburg Rules, formally known as the United Nations Convention on the Carriage of Goods by Sea, 1978, were developed in response to growing dissatisfaction with the Hague-Visby Rules. The primary criticism of the Hague-Visby Rules was that they heavily favored carriers at the expense of shippers. In an effort to create a more equitable framework, the Hamburg Rules aimed to redress the balance of responsibilities and liabilities between carriers and shippers. The Hamburg Rules came into force on November 1, 1992, after achieving the necessary number of ratifications.

Extended Carrier Liability Period

One of the most significant changes introduced by the Hamburg Rules is the extension of the carrier's liability period. Under the Hague-Visby Rules, carrier liability typically begins when the goods cross the ship's rail and ends when they are discharged. The Hamburg Rules, however, extend the carrier's liability from the time they take charge of the goods until delivery. This change addresses the period when goods are often most vulnerable and ensures that carriers are responsible for the entire transit process.

Simplified Claims Procedure

The Hamburg Rules also simplify the procedure for making claims against carriers. Under the Hague-Visby Rules, shippers often face complex and cumbersome processes to prove liability and recover damages. The Hamburg Rules streamline these procedures, making it easier for shippers to file claims and seek compensation. This simplification is intended to reduce the legal and administrative burdens on shippers, providing them with a more straightforward path to redress.

Increased Carrier Responsibilities

The Hamburg Rules place greater responsibilities on carriers, including stricter obligations to ensure the seaworthiness of the vessel and the proper handling and stowage of goods. These enhanced responsibilities aim to promote higher standards of care and diligence among carriers, thereby reducing the incidence of damage and loss. By imposing these stricter requirements, the Hamburg Rules seek to enhance the overall safety and reliability of maritime transportation.

Liability for Delay

Another significant aspect of the Hamburg Rules is the introduction of carrier liability for delay in the delivery of goods. Under the Hague-Visby Rules, carriers are generally not liable for delays unless the delay causes physical damage to the goods. The Hamburg Rules, however, recognize the financial impact of delays on shippers and provide for compensation in cases where the delay causes loss or damage. This provision is particularly relevant in modern just-in-time logistics systems, where timely delivery is critical.

Wider Applicability

The Hamburg Rules have a broader scope of application compared to the Hague-Visby Rules. They apply to all contracts of carriage by sea, except those explicitly excluded, such as charter parties and certain types of specialized transport. This wider applicability ensures that the Hamburg Rules cover a greater range of maritime transactions, providing more comprehensive protection for shippers and a more uniform legal framework for maritime trade.

Limited Adoption

Despite their progressive provisions, the Hamburg Rules have not been widely adopted. As of now, relatively few countries have ratified the convention, with the majority of maritime nations continuing to adhere to the Hague-Visby Rules or transitioning to the Rotterdam Rules. The limited adoption can be attributed to various factors, including resistance from the shipping industry, which may view the increased liabilities and responsibilities as burdensome.

Industry Resistance

The shipping industry's resistance to the Hamburg Rules stems from concerns about the increased costs and liabilities associated with the new framework. Carriers argue that the stricter liability provisions and extended liability period could lead to higher insurance premiums and operational costs. Additionally, the potential for increased litigation and claims may deter carriers from supporting the Hamburg Rules, preferring the more carrier-friendly provisions of the Hague-Visby Rules.

Comparative Analysis with the Rotterdam Rules

The Rotterdam Rules, adopted in 2008, aim to modernize and expand the scope of maritime law, incorporating elements from both the Hague-Visby and Hamburg Rules. The Rotterdam Rules address some of the limitations of the Hamburg Rules by providing a more balanced framework that also covers multimodal transport. However, like the Hamburg Rules, the Rotterdam Rules face challenges in achieving widespread adoption, highlighting the complexities of achieving global consensus in maritime law.

Future Prospects and Recommendations

The future of the Hamburg Rules remains uncertain. For the Hamburg Rules to gain wider acceptance, there must be concerted efforts to address the concerns of the shipping industry and demonstrate the benefits of the new framework. This could involve promoting the advantages of enhanced shipper protection and the potential for improved safety and reliability in maritime transport. Additionally, fostering greater international cooperation and dialogue among stakeholders is crucial to achieving broader ratification and implementation of the Hamburg Rules. By addressing these challenges, the Hamburg Rules can play a more significant role in shaping a fair and equitable legal framework for international maritime trade.

Rotterdam Rules :

Introduction to the Rotterdam Rules

The Rotterdam Rules, formally titled the United Nations Convention on Contracts for the International Carriage of Goods Wholly or Partly by Sea, were adopted in 2008. They represent the latest attempt to modernize and harmonize international maritime law. The Rules aim to address the shortcomings of previous conventions, such as the Hague-Visby Rules and the Hamburg Rules, by covering a broader range of transport contracts, including multimodal transport and electronic commerce. Despite their comprehensive scope, the Rotterdam Rules have faced challenges in achieving widespread adoption.

Comprehensive Coverage of Transport Contracts

One of the most significant advancements of the Rotterdam Rules is their comprehensive coverage of transport contracts. Unlike their predecessors, the Rotterdam Rules extend beyond maritime transport to include multimodal transportation, where goods are carried by different modes of transport under a single contract. This broader scope reflects the realities of modern logistics and supply chain management, where goods often move seamlessly across multiple transport modes.

Provisions for Electronic Commerce

The Rotterdam Rules are also notable for incorporating provisions for electronic commerce. Recognizing the growing importance of digital transactions in international trade, the Rules facilitate the use of electronic transport documents and electronic communications. This modernization aims to enhance efficiency, reduce paperwork, and streamline the documentation process, aligning maritime law with contemporary business practices.

Enhanced Shipper and Carrier Responsibilities

The Rotterdam Rules attempt to balance the interests of shippers and carriers by enhancing the responsibilities and liabilities of both parties. For instance, the Rules impose stricter obligations on carriers to ensure the seaworthiness of vessels and the proper handling of goods. At the same time, shippers are required to provide accurate information about the cargo and comply with packing and labeling requirements. This dual approach aims to promote greater accountability and reduce the incidence of disputes.

Extended Liability Periods

Another critical feature of the Rotterdam Rules is the extension of the carrier's liability period. Under previous conventions, carrier liability typically ended when the goods were discharged from the vessel. The Rotterdam Rules, however, extend this liability to cover the entire transport period, from the time the carrier receives the goods until delivery. This extension provides greater protection for shippers and aligns with the principles of modern logistics, where end-to-end responsibility is increasingly important.

Limited Adoption and Ratification

Despite their innovative provisions, the Rotterdam Rules have struggled to gain widespread adoption. As of now, relatively few countries have ratified the convention. This limited adoption can be attributed to various factors, including resistance from the shipping industry, which may perceive the increased liabilities and responsibilities as burdensome. Additionally, the transition from existing frameworks, such as the Hague-Visby Rules, to the Rotterdam Rules involves significant legal and administrative adjustments, which can be daunting for many countries.

Industry Resistance and Concerns

The shipping industry's resistance to the Rotterdam Rules is a major barrier to their adoption. Carriers express concerns about the increased costs and liabilities associated with the new framework. The extended liability period and stricter obligations could lead to higher insurance premiums and operational costs. Additionally, the potential for increased litigation and claims may deter carriers from supporting the Rotterdam Rules, preferring the more familiar and established provisions of the Hague-Visby Rules.

Comparative Analysis with Previous Conventions

A comparative analysis with previous conventions highlights the strengths and limitations of the Rotterdam Rules. While the Rules address many of the deficiencies of the Hague-Visby and Hamburg Rules, such as outdated provisions and limited scope, they also introduce complexities that can be challenging to implement. The broader coverage and electronic commerce provisions are significant advancements, but the increased responsibilities and liabilities may not be appealing to all stakeholders.

Potential for Future Adoption

The future adoption of the Rotterdam Rules depends on several factors, including international cooperation and the perceived benefits of the new framework. For the Rules to gain wider acceptance, there must be concerted efforts to address the concerns of the shipping industry and demonstrate the advantages of enhanced shipper protection and improved logistics efficiency. Education and awareness programs can also play a crucial role in promoting the Rules and facilitating their implementation.

Conclusion and Future Prospects

In conclusion, the Rotterdam Rules represent a significant step forward in the modernization and harmonization of international maritime law. Their comprehensive coverage of transport contracts and provisions for electronic commerce address the needs of contemporary logistics and supply chain management. However, the limited adoption and resistance from the shipping industry highlight the challenges of transitioning to a new legal framework. Future efforts should focus on promoting the benefits of the Rotterdam Rules, addressing industry concerns, and fostering international cooperation to achieve broader ratification and implementation. By doing so, the Rotterdam Rules can play a pivotal role in shaping a fair and efficient legal framework for the international carriage of goods by sea.

Encyclopedia — **THE PATRON** — .285

TOPIC 2:

Bills of Lading and Their Legal Implications

Marwan M. Alarjan — **MASTR** — Martin Apollo Bureau

Introduction to Bills of Lading

Bills of lading are indispensable in the maritime industry, acting as pivotal instruments in the shipping process. These documents encapsulate critical information about the goods being transported, the terms of shipment, and the responsibilities of both the shipper and the carrier. As maritime trade underpins a substantial portion of global commerce, understanding the legal implications of bills of lading is essential for smooth and efficient international trade.

Historical Context and Evolution

The concept of the bill of lading dates back to medieval times when merchants needed a reliable means to document the receipt and transport of goods. Over the centuries, bills of lading have evolved from simple receipts to sophisticated legal documents that play a central role in modern maritime law. Their development reflects the growing complexity and internationalization of maritime trade, necessitating standardized practices to facilitate global commerce.

Function as a Receipt

One of the primary functions of a bill of lading is to serve as a receipt for the goods shipped. This document confirms that the carrier has received the goods as described by the shipper and in the condition noted. This receipt function is crucial for both parties; it provides shippers with proof that the carrier has taken custody of the goods, and it protects carriers by documenting the state of the goods at the time of receipt, thereby limiting their liability for pre-existing damage or discrepancies.

Evidence of the Contract of Carriage

A bill of lading also serves as evidence of the contract of carriage between the shipper and the carrier. This aspect outlines the terms and conditions under which the goods are transported, including the obligations and liabilities of each party. By codifying these terms, the bill of lading provides a clear framework for resolving disputes and enforcing contractual obligations, thus ensuring that both shippers and carriers adhere to agreed-upon standards.

Document of Title

Perhaps the most critical function of a bill of lading is its role as a document of title. This means that the holder of the bill of lading has the right to claim ownership of the goods and can transfer this right to others. This feature is vital for facilitating trade, as it allows goods to be bought and sold while in transit. The transferability of bills of lading underpins the liquidity of goods in international trade, enabling merchants to engage in transactions without having to physically handle the goods.

Legal Implications for Carriers

For carriers, issuing a bill of lading carries significant legal implications. They are bound by the terms specified in the document, including liability for loss or damage to the goods during transport. Carriers must ensure the accuracy of the information in the bill of lading, as any discrepancies can lead to disputes and potential legal claims. The obligations imposed by bills of lading require carriers to adopt meticulous practices in handling and documenting shipments.

Legal Implications for Shippers

Shippers also face important legal considerations related to bills of lading. These documents are critical for asserting rights against carriers and for facilitating the transfer of goods. Shippers must ensure that the bill of lading accurately reflects the terms of the contract of carriage and the condition of the goods. Inaccuracies or omissions can undermine their ability to enforce their rights and can lead to complications in the transfer of ownership.

Disputes involving bills of lading can arise over various issues, such as misdelivery, fraud, or discrepancies in the goods' description. Effective dispute resolution mechanisms are essential for addressing these conflicts. Arbitration and litigation are common methods for resolving disputes related to bills of lading, and the choice of forum often depends on the specific terms outlined in the document. The enforceability of arbitration awards and court judgments underpins the reliability of dispute resolution processes in maritime trade.

Electronic Bills of Lading (eBLs)

The rise of digital technology has introduced electronic bills of lading (eBLs), which offer several advantages over traditional paper documents, such as increased efficiency and reduced risk of fraud. However, the adoption of eBLs also raises new legal questions, including the recognition of digital signatures and the legal status of electronic documents. Ensuring that eBLs comply with international standards and are accepted by all parties involved is crucial for their effective implementation.

In conclusion, bills of lading are multifaceted documents with significant legal implications for both carriers and shippers. They function as receipts for goods, evidence of contracts of carriage, and documents of title, each role carrying distinct responsibilities and risks. As international trade continues to evolve, particularly with the advent of digitalization, the legal framework governing bills of lading must adapt to ensure clarity, efficiency, and security in maritime commerce. A thorough understanding of the legal implications of bills of lading is essential for stakeholders to navigate the complexities of international trade and to facilitate smooth and predictable commercial transactions.

Functions of a Bill of Lading

1. Receipt of Goods

The function of a bill of lading as a receipt of goods is fundamental in the shipping process. When a carrier issues a bill of lading, it confirms that the goods described in the document have been received from the shipper in the specified condition. This acknowledgment serves several practical purposes:

- **Verification and Accountability:** The receipt function provides a verifiable record that the carrier has taken possession of the goods, detailing their quantity, quality, and condition at the time of receipt. This helps to establish accountability and can be critical in resolving disputes over the condition of goods upon delivery.
- **Evidence for Claims:** In the event of damage or loss during transit, the bill of lading serves as a key piece of evidence for the shipper to file a claim against the carrier. It documents the state of the goods at the start of the journey, thereby supporting claims for compensation if the goods are not delivered in the same condition.

- **Inventory Management:** For shippers and carriers, the receipt function assists in inventory management by providing an official record of what has been handed over for transport. This can be particularly important in large-scale shipping operations where multiple shipments are managed simultaneously.

2. Evidence of Contract

As evidence of the contract of carriage, a bill of lading outlines the terms and conditions agreed upon by the shipper and the carrier. This function has several practical implications:

- **Contractual Clarity:** The bill of lading explicitly states the obligations of both parties, including delivery terms, payment conditions, and liability clauses. This clarity helps prevent misunderstandings and disputes, ensuring that both parties are aware of their responsibilities.
- **Legal Enforceability:** In case of a breach of contract, the bill of lading can be presented in court or arbitration proceedings as proof of the agreed terms. This makes it easier to enforce the contract and seek remedies for non-compliance, such as damages or specific performance.

- **Risk Management:** By specifying the terms of carriage, the bill of lading helps both parties manage risks associated with the transport of goods. For instance, it can include provisions for handling hazardous materials, perishable goods, or special handling requirements, thereby reducing the likelihood of disputes and ensuring compliance with regulations.

3. Document of Title

The role of a bill of lading as a document of title is particularly significant in the context of international trade, where the transfer of ownership and possession of goods needs to be managed efficiently. Practical implications include:

- **Facilitating Trade Financing:** Banks and financial institutions often require a bill of lading as collateral for issuing letters of credit or other forms of trade finance. The document of title function enables shippers to obtain financing by pledging the goods in transit as security, thus facilitating smoother and more secure trade transactions.
- **Transfer of Ownership:** The bill of lading allows the holder to transfer ownership of the goods by endorsing the document to another party. This feature is crucial in

supply chain management, where goods may change hands multiple times before reaching the final buyer. It ensures that the rightful owner has the authority to claim the goods upon delivery.

- **Simplifying Logistics:** For international shipments, the bill of lading helps streamline the logistics of transferring goods between multiple parties. It provides a standardized method for proving ownership and right of possession, reducing the complexity and administrative burden associated with cross-border trade.

Practical Scenario Example:

Imagine a scenario where a manufacturer in China ships electronic components to a distributor in the United States. The manufacturer issues a bill of lading to the carrier, which acknowledges receipt of the goods. The bill of lading details the contract terms, such as delivery date, handling requirements, and payment conditions. During transit, the distributor secures trade financing from a bank by presenting the bill of lading as collateral. Upon arrival at the destination port, the bill of lading, as a document of title, allows the distributor to take possession of the goods and transfer ownership to downstream buyers if necessary. This seamless process highlights the practical importance of the bill of lading in facilitating efficient and secure international trade.

By serving as a receipt of goods, evidence of contract, and document of title, the bill of lading plays a critical role in managing and mitigating risks, ensuring legal compliance, and streamlining logistics in international shipping. Understanding these functions and their practical implications is essential for businesses to navigate the complexities of global trade effectively.

Types of Bills of Lading

1. Straight Bill of Lading

A straight bill of lading is non-negotiable and is issued to a specific consignee named in the document. This type of bill of lading has several practical applications and implications:

- **Security and Specificity:** Since a straight bill of lading is issued to a named consignee, it provides a higher level of security by ensuring that only the specified recipient can claim the goods. This can be particularly important for high-value shipments or where the shipper wants to control precisely who receives the goods.

- **Simplified Transactions:** The non-negotiable nature of a straight bill of lading simplifies the transaction process as there is no need for endorsements or transfers. This can reduce administrative burdens and streamline the logistics process, particularly in domestic or straightforward international transactions.

- **Reduced Risk of Fraud:** Because the consignee is explicitly named and the bill cannot be transferred to another party, the risk of fraudulent claims is minimized.

This can be crucial for shipments where the security and integrity of the delivery process are paramount.

Practical Scenario Example: Consider a scenario where a pharmaceutical company in Germany ships a batch of vaccines to a specific hospital in Brazil. The company issues a straight bill of lading naming the hospital as the consignee. This ensures that the vaccines can only be claimed by the designated hospital, providing security and ensuring that the sensitive shipment reaches its intended recipient without complications.

2. Order Bill of Lading

An order bill of lading is negotiable and can be endorsed and transferred to others, making it highly versatile in international trade:

- **Flexibility in Trade:** The negotiable nature of an order bill of lading allows it to be endorsed and transferred multiple times during the shipment process. This flexibility is particularly beneficial in complex supply chains where goods may be sold and resold several times before reaching the final buyer.

- **Facilitating Financing:** Order bills of lading are commonly used in trade financing. Banks and financial institutions accept them as collateral for issuing letters of credit or other financial instruments, thereby facilitating international trade. The ability to endorse and transfer the bill increases its utility in securing financing and managing liquidity.
- **Enhanced Marketability:** The negotiable nature of an order bill of lading enhances the marketability of the goods, as it allows the holder to transfer ownership easily. This can be advantageous in industries where goods are frequently traded in transit, such as commodities or electronics.

Practical Scenario Example: Imagine a situation where a trader in Singapore purchases a bulk shipment of coffee beans from a supplier in Colombia and plans to sell the beans to various buyers in Europe. An order bill of lading is issued, allowing the trader to endorse and transfer the bill to the European buyers while the goods are still in transit. This flexibility facilitates the trader's ability to manage sales and finances efficiently.

3. Bearer Bill of Lading

A bearer bill of lading is transferable by delivery without endorsement, making it highly fluid and convenient in certain trade scenarios:

- **Ease of Transfer:** The most significant advantage of a bearer bill of lading is the ease of transfer. The holder of the bill can claim the goods upon delivery simply by presenting the document. This can be particularly useful in trades involving bulk or fungible goods, where ownership may change frequently.
- **Reduced Documentation Requirements:** Since no endorsement is required to transfer a bearer bill of lading, the administrative and documentation requirements are minimized. This can expedite the transfer process and reduce delays, especially in fast-moving trades or high-volume shipments.
- **Flexibility for Short-Term Trade:** Bearer bills of lading are often used in short-term trades where goods need to change hands quickly and with minimal procedural requirements. This can be beneficial in markets where speed and flexibility are critical.

Practical Scenario Example: Consider a case where a bulk shipment of grain is being transported from Argentina to multiple buyers in various countries. A bearer bill of lading is issued, allowing the initial buyer to sell portions of the grain to different buyers along the route. Each new buyer can claim their portion of the shipment upon presentation of the bearer bill, facilitating a seamless and flexible trading process.

Conclusion:

Understanding the practical implications of different types of bills of lading is crucial for businesses engaged in international trade. The choice between a straight, order, or bearer bill of lading depends on the specific needs of the transaction, including security requirements, financing needs, and the nature of the goods being shipped. By selecting the appropriate type of bill of lading, businesses can optimize their logistics, enhance security, and facilitate smoother trade operations.

Legal Implications

1. Liabilities

The carrier's liability for loss or damage to goods is a critical legal implication of bills of lading and is typically governed by international conventions such as the Hague-Visby Rules:

- **Hague-Visby Rules:** These rules set out the minimum standards for the carrier's responsibility and liability for loss or damage to goods during transit. Under these rules, carriers are liable for any loss, damage, or delay in the delivery of goods unless they can prove that the loss was due to an excepted cause, such as an act of God, war, or inherent defect of the goods.
- **Practical Application:** Shippers and consignees need to be aware of these liabilities to effectively manage risks. For instance, a shipper should ensure that the carrier complies with the Hague-Visby Rules to secure compensation in case of loss or damage. Additionally, carriers should maintain robust documentation and evidence to defend against claims by proving excepted causes.

- **Insurance Considerations:** Given the liabilities involved, both carriers and shippers often secure marine insurance to cover potential losses. Understanding the extent of carrier liability and the scope of insurance coverage is crucial for risk management in maritime trade.

Practical Scenario Example: A manufacturer in China ships electronics to a retailer in the United States. During transit, the goods are damaged due to rough seas. The retailer can claim compensation from the carrier under the Hague-Visby Rules, provided that the damage was not caused by an excepted peril. The manufacturer can also rely on marine insurance to cover the losses.

2. Rights of Holders

The holder of a bill of lading has specific rights that are crucial for the execution of maritime trade contracts:

- **Right to Claim Delivery:** The holder of a bill of lading has the right to claim delivery of the goods upon arrival at the destination. This right ensures that the consignee or lawful holder can take possession of the goods without unnecessary delays or disputes.

- **Legal Recourse:** The holder can sue the carrier for breach of contract if the goods are not delivered as per the terms of the bill of lading. This right provides a legal mechanism to enforce contractual obligations and seek compensation for any losses incurred due to the carrier's failure to deliver the goods in the agreed condition.
- **Transfer of Rights:** In the case of order or bearer bills of lading, these rights can be transferred through endorsement or delivery, allowing subsequent holders to claim delivery and enforce the contract.

Practical Scenario Example: A furniture exporter in Italy ships goods to a distributor in Canada under an order bill of lading. The distributor, in turn, sells the goods to a retailer in the United States while the shipment is in transit. By endorsing the bill of lading to the retailer, the distributor transfers the right to claim the goods and sue the carrier if necessary.

3. Transferability

The transferability of bills of lading has significant practical implications for international trade and finance:

- **Negotiable Instruments:** Order and bearer bills of lading are negotiable, meaning they can be endorsed and transferred to other parties. This transferability is essential for the flexibility and fluidity of maritime trade, allowing the ownership of goods to change hands while they are in transit.

- **Collateral for Financing:** The negotiable nature of bills of lading allows them to be used as collateral in financial transactions. Banks and financial institutions accept them as security for loans and letters of credit, facilitating trade finance. This capability is crucial for exporters and importers who need financing to manage cash flow and business operations.

- **Practical Considerations:** Businesses should carefully manage the endorsement and transfer of bills of lading to ensure that the chain of title is clear and enforceable. Proper documentation and adherence to legal requirements are essential to avoid disputes and ensure the smooth execution of trade and financing agreements.

Practical Scenario Example: A textile exporter in India ships goods to a buyer in Europe under an order bill of lading. The exporter needs immediate cash flow to manage operations and approaches a bank for a loan. By endorsing the bill of lading to the bank as collateral, the exporter secures the necessary financing. The bank, in turn, has the right to claim the goods or transfer the bill to another party if the exporter defaults on the loan.

Conclusion

The legal implications of bills of lading encompass liabilities, rights of holders, and transferability, all of which play a crucial role in maritime trade. Understanding these aspects helps businesses manage risks, enforce contractual rights, and utilize bills of lading as financial instruments. Proper management of these legal implications ensures smooth and efficient international trade operations, supporting the global flow of goods and capital.

TOPIC 3:

Liability of Carriers and Shippers

Carrier's Liability

1. Period of Responsibility

The carrier's liability typically begins when they take charge of the goods and ends upon delivery. This period is crucial for determining the extent of the carrier's responsibility and the point at which risk transfers from the carrier to the consignee:

- **Taking Charge of Goods:** The period of responsibility starts when the carrier takes physical possession of the goods, often at the port of loading. It is essential for shippers to ensure that the goods are properly documented and inspected at this stage to establish a clear record of their condition.

- **Delivery of Goods:** The carrier's responsibility ends upon delivery to the consignee at the destination port. To avoid disputes, consignees should promptly inspect the goods upon arrival and document any discrepancies or damages. This documentation serves as evidence in case of claims against the carrier.

Practical Scenario Example: A logistics company in Brazil ships coffee beans to a buyer in Germany. The carrier's liability period starts when the goods are loaded onto the vessel in Brazil and ends when they are unloaded in Germany. If the coffee beans are damaged during transit, the carrier may be held liable for the damage, provided the damage occurred within this period.

2. Limits of Liability

International conventions often set monetary limits on the carrier's liability per package or per unit of weight. These limits are designed to provide a balance between protecting the interests of shippers and controlling the risks for carriers:

- **Monetary Limits:** The Hague-Visby Rules, for example, set limits on the carrier's liability, often calculated per package or unit of weight (e.g., SDR per kilogram). This limit provides a predictable framework for compensation in case of loss or damage.
- **Practical Implications:** Shippers should be aware of these liability limits and consider additional insurance if the value of their goods exceeds the carrier's liability

limit. This awareness ensures that they are adequately compensated in case of significant losses.

Practical Scenario Example: An electronics manufacturer in Japan ships high-value computer components to a distributor in Canada. The components are worth significantly more than the liability limit set by the Hague-Visby Rules. To cover the excess value, the manufacturer takes out additional cargo insurance. If the components are damaged, the insurance will cover the difference between the actual value and the carrier's liability limit.

3. Exceptions to Liability

Carriers may be exempt from liability under certain conditions, such as acts of God, acts of war, or negligence of the shipper. These exceptions are critical for understanding the limitations of carrier liability:

- **Acts of God:** Natural disasters such as storms, earthquakes, or floods that are beyond the control of the carrier. If the damage to the goods is caused by such events, the carrier may be exempt from liability.

- **Acts of War:** Situations involving war, piracy, or other hostile actions that could impact the safety of the goods during transit. Carriers are generally not liable for losses due to these extraordinary circumstances.
- **Negligence of the Shipper:** If the shipper's negligence contributes to the loss or damage of goods, such as improper packaging or incorrect documentation, the carrier may not be held liable. Shippers must ensure that their goods are properly prepared and documented to avoid this exemption.

Practical Scenario Example: A furniture exporter in Italy ships goods to the United States. During transit, a severe storm damages the ship and the cargo. Since the storm is considered an act of God, the carrier may be exempt from liability for the damaged furniture. To mitigate such risks, the exporter should ensure adequate insurance coverage for their shipments.

Conclusion

Understanding the carrier's liability, including the period of responsibility, limits of liability, and exceptions, is essential for managing risks in maritime trade. Proper documentation, additional insurance, and awareness of potential exceptions can help shippers and consignees navigate the complexities of carrier liability and ensure that their interests are protected throughout the shipping process. This comprehensive approach to managing carrier liability ensures smoother and more predictable international trade transactions.

Shipper's Liability

1. Proper Declaration

Accurately declaring the nature, weight, and value of goods is a critical responsibility for shippers under maritime law. This ensures that the carrier can plan appropriately for the transportation and handling of the cargo, reducing the risk of damage and delays:

- **Nature of Goods:** Detailed descriptions of the goods being shipped help carriers understand any special handling or storage requirements. This is especially important for perishable or fragile items.
- **Weight of Goods:** Accurate weight declarations ensure that the ship is not overloaded and that weight distribution is managed to maintain the vessel's stability. Incorrect weight declarations can lead to serious safety risks.
- **Value of Goods:** Declaring the correct value of the goods is essential for insurance purposes and for calculating potential liabilities. It also affects the duties and taxes assessed by customs authorities.

Practical Scenario Example: A textile exporter in India ships a container of fabrics to the UK. The exporter provides an accurate declaration of the nature of the goods (e.g., type of fabric, weight, and value). This information helps the carrier handle the container correctly, ensuring safe transportation and facilitating smooth customs clearance upon arrival.

2. Packaging and Labeling

Proper packaging and labeling of goods are essential to protect them from damage during sea transport. Effective packaging ensures that the goods can withstand the various stresses encountered during loading, transit, and unloading:

- **Durable Packaging:** Using robust materials and methods to package goods can prevent physical damage. For example, crating, palletizing, and using moisture-resistant materials are common practices.
- **Correct Labeling:** Labels should clearly indicate handling instructions, the nature of the goods, and any hazards. Labels also help in the efficient and safe stacking and storage of cargo.

- **Protection Against Elements:** Packaging should also protect goods from exposure to saltwater, humidity, and temperature changes, which are common in maritime environments.

Practical Scenario Example: A company in Brazil exports electronics to Australia. The electronics are packaged in shock-absorbent materials and moisture-proof containers. Labels indicating "fragile" and "this side up" are prominently displayed. This ensures that the goods are handled with care, reducing the risk of damage during the long sea journey.

3. Compliance with Regulations

Shippers must ensure that they comply with all relevant regulations, including those related to dangerous goods. Non-compliance can lead to legal penalties, delays, and increased liability in case of incidents:

- **Dangerous Goods Regulations:** Specific rules govern the transport of hazardous materials, including proper labeling, documentation, and packaging. Shippers must be aware of and comply with these regulations to prevent accidents.

- **Customs Regulations:** Accurate documentation and compliance with customs regulations are crucial for the smooth entry and exit of goods at ports. This includes adhering to import/export restrictions and tariff requirements.

- **Environmental Regulations:** Compliance with environmental regulations, such as those addressing the disposal of packaging materials and the handling of hazardous substances, is increasingly important.

Practical Scenario Example: A chemicals manufacturer in Germany ships industrial solvents to China. The manufacturer adheres to international dangerous goods regulations, ensuring that the solvents are packaged in certified containers and labeled with the appropriate hazard warnings. Detailed documentation is provided to the carrier and customs authorities, facilitating safe handling and compliance with regulatory requirements.

Conclusion

Shippers play a crucial role in ensuring the safe and efficient transport of goods by sea. Proper declaration, packaging, labeling, and regulatory compliance are key responsibilities that help prevent damage, delays, and legal issues. By understanding and fulfilling their liabilities, shippers contribute to the overall reliability and safety of maritime trade. This proactive approach to managing shipper responsibilities helps build trust with carriers, reduces risks, and ensures smooth international shipping operations.

TOPIC 4:

Recent Developments and Case Studies

The maritime industry has seen significant technological advancements in recent years, including the adoption of digital tools and automated systems. These developments have had profound implications for maritime law, particularly in areas such as electronic documentation, cybersecurity, and autonomous shipping:

1. Electronic Documentation:

The transition from paper-based to electronic documentation has streamlined many processes in maritime trade. Electronic bills of lading (eBL) are increasingly used, providing quicker and more secure transactions. Legal frameworks have evolved to accommodate these changes, ensuring that electronic documents are given the same legal standing as their paper counterparts.

- **Cybersecurity:** As ships and ports become more connected, the risk of cyber-attacks increases. Maritime law now encompasses regulations and guidelines aimed at enhancing cybersecurity measures. For example, the International Maritime Organization (IMO) has issued guidelines to protect maritime cyber resilience, highlighting the need for shipowners and operators to implement robust cybersecurity practices.

- **Autonomous Shipping:** The development of autonomous ships presents both opportunities and challenges. Maritime law is adapting to address issues such as liability, navigation, and safety standards for unmanned vessels.

Regulatory bodies are working on creating frameworks that balance innovation with safety and accountability.

Case Study: Electronic Bills of Lading

A major shipping company implemented an eBL system to reduce administrative costs and improve efficiency. This system allowed for the instantaneous transfer of ownership and reduced the risk of fraud. Legal adjustments were made to recognize eBLs under national and international law, providing the necessary legal assurances for widespread adoption.

2. Environmental Regulations

Environmental concerns have led to stricter regulations in maritime law, focusing on reducing pollution and protecting marine ecosystems. The IMO has been at the forefront of these initiatives, introducing several key regulations:

- **MARPOL Annex VI:** The International Convention for the Prevention of Pollution from Ships (MARPOL) Annex VI sets limits on sulfur emissions from ships. Recent amendments have tightened these limits, requiring ships to use low-sulfur fuel or install exhaust cleaning systems (scrubbers).

- **Ballast Water Management Convention:** This convention aims to prevent the spread of invasive aquatic species through ships' ballast water. It requires ships to manage their ballast water and sediments according to specific standards and procedures.

Case Study: Implementation of Low-Sulfur Fuel Regulations

A global shipping company faced challenges in complying with the new sulfur emission limits. The company invested in scrubbers and transitioned to low-sulfur fuel, incurring significant costs. However, compliance with the regulations not only avoided legal penalties but also enhanced the company's reputation as an environmentally responsible operator.

3. Trade Practices and Economic Shifts

Global trade practices and economic shifts have influenced recent developments in maritime law. The increasing complexity of international trade, combined with economic fluctuations, has led to changes in how maritime contracts are structured and enforced:

- **Trade Wars and Tariffs:** Trade disputes and the imposition of tariffs have led to disruptions in global shipping routes and changes in contractual terms. Maritime contracts now often include clauses that address the impact of tariffs and trade restrictions on shipping operations.

- **COVID-19 Pandemic:** The pandemic significantly affected global shipping, causing delays and disruptions. Maritime law adapted by addressing issues such as crew changes, quarantine regulations, and force majeure clauses in contracts.

Case Study: Impact of COVID-19 on Maritime Contracts

During the COVID-19 pandemic, a shipping company invoked the force majeure clause in its contracts due to port closures and quarantine measures. The legal interpretation of force majeure in this context was critical in determining the company's liability for delayed deliveries. Courts and arbitral tribunals considered the unprecedented nature of the pandemic in their rulings, highlighting the importance of flexibility in maritime contracts.

4. Regulatory Changes and International Cooperation

International cooperation and regulatory changes continue to shape maritime law. The IMO, along with regional organizations, has played a key role in developing new regulations and promoting harmonization:

- **Polar Code:** The IMO's Polar Code sets mandatory standards for ships operating in polar waters, addressing safety and environmental protection. This code is a response to the increasing commercial activity in the Arctic and Antarctic regions due to climate change and melting ice caps.

- **EU Regulations:** The European Union has introduced several regulations impacting maritime law, such as the Ship Recycling Regulation, which ensures that ships are recycled in an environmentally sound manner, and the Monitoring, Reporting, and Verification (MRV) Regulation for CO_2 emissions from ships.

Case Study: Compliance with the Polar Code

A shipping company operating in the Arctic region had to upgrade its fleet to comply with the Polar Code's safety and environmental requirements. This involved significant investments in ship modifications and crew training. The regulatory changes aimed to minimize the environmental impact of shipping in vulnerable polar regions while ensuring the safety of operations in harsh conditions.

5. Legal Precedents and Case Law

Recent case law continues to shape the interpretation and application of maritime law. Courts and arbitration panels around the world have addressed various issues, providing clarity and setting precedents for future cases:

- **Liability and Compensation:** Legal cases involving oil spills, collisions, and cargo damage have further defined the scope of liability and compensation under maritime law. These cases often involve complex interpretations of international conventions and national laws.

- **Dispute Resolution:** Arbitration remains a preferred method for resolving maritime disputes. Recent arbitral awards have addressed issues such as charter party disputes, contract interpretation, and enforcement of arbitral decisions.

Case Study: Arbitration in Charter Party Disputes

A dispute between a shipowner and a charterer over the interpretation of a charter party agreement was resolved through arbitration. The arbitration panel's decision provided valuable insights into the contractual obligations and highlighted the importance of clear and precise contract terms in avoiding disputes.

6. Future Trends and Prospects

Looking ahead, maritime law will continue to evolve in response to technological, environmental, and economic changes. Key areas of focus include:

- **Sustainability:** The push for greener shipping practices will drive further regulatory changes aimed at reducing the environmental footprint of maritime activities.

- **Digitalization:** Continued advancements in digital technology will impact maritime law, particularly in areas such as cybersecurity, electronic documentation, and autonomous shipping.

- **Global Cooperation:** Enhanced international cooperation will be essential for addressing global challenges, such as climate change and maritime security, and ensuring the smooth operation of international maritime trade.

Conclusion

Recent developments in maritime law reflect the dynamic nature of the global shipping industry. Technological advancements, environmental concerns, changes in trade practices, and regulatory shifts are all driving the evolution of maritime law. Case studies provide practical insights into how these developments impact the interpretation and application of maritime law, highlighting the importance of continuous adaptation and innovation in this critical field. As the industry evolves, maritime law will need to keep pace, ensuring that it provides a robust and flexible framework for international maritime trade.

Encyclopedia   - **THE PATRON** -   .330

MAIN CASE STUDIES . . .

Marwan M. Alarjan   - **MASTR** -   Martin Apollo Bureau

Case Study: The Ever Given Incident

Background and Context

In March 2021, the Ever Given, a large container ship operated by Evergreen Marine, became lodged in the Suez Canal, blocking the vital maritime artery for six days. The Suez Canal is one of the world's most important trade routes, accounting for about 12% of global trade. The blockage created a significant bottleneck, affecting nearly 400 ships and leading to substantial economic and logistical disruptions worldwide.

Carrier Liability

The incident raised critical questions about the liability of the carrier. According to maritime law, carriers are generally responsible for ensuring the safe passage of goods. The blockage of the canal caused significant delays and financial losses for the companies whose goods were on board the Ever Given and the ships delayed by the incident.

- **Legal Framework:** Under the Hague-Visby Rules, which govern many aspects of international shipping, the carrier is liable for damage or loss unless it can prove that the incident was caused by an exception, such as an act of God, an act of war, or navigational errors. In the case of the Ever Given, determining liability was complex. The ship's operator, Evergreen Marine, claimed that strong winds and poor visibility due to a sandstorm caused the grounding. However, questions about potential human error and whether the crew adhered to standard navigational practices were also considered.

- **Jurisprudence and Precedents:** Similar cases have seen courts analyze the extent to which environmental conditions and human error contribute to such incidents. For instance, in *The Hellenic Lines Ltd. v. Mr. Justices of Appeal of the Queen's Bench*, the court held that the carrier must demonstrate due diligence in ensuring the ship's seaworthiness and proper navigation. The findings in the Ever Given case would likely hinge on similar considerations.

General Average

The principle of General Average, a foundational concept in maritime law, was invoked following the Ever Given incident. General Average requires all parties with a financial interest in the maritime venture to proportionately share the losses resulting from a voluntary and successful sacrifice of part of the ship or cargo to save the whole in an emergency.

- **Application in the Ever Given Case:** The costs of refloating the vessel, repairing the canal, and any cargo damage were substantial. Under General Average, these costs were distributed among the shipowner, cargo owners, and other stakeholders. This principle aims to ensure that no single party bears the entire burden of extraordinary losses incurred for the common benefit of all parties involved in the voyage.

- **Legal Analysis:** Historically, the application of General Average has been reaffirmed in cases such as *The Strathclyde* (1876), where the court supported the equitable sharing of losses. The Ever Given incident reiterated the relevance of this ancient principle in modern maritime commerce, showcasing its importance in managing financial risks in large-scale shipping operations.

Insurance Claims

The incident resulted in numerous insurance claims, reflecting the critical role of comprehensive marine insurance coverage in mitigating financial risks associated with maritime accidents.

- **Types of Insurance Involved:**

    o **Hull and Machinery Insurance:** This covers physical damage to the ship. The Ever Given's owners would have likely filed claims under this policy for the costs of refloating and repairing the vessel.

    o **Cargo Insurance:** Cargo owners affected by delays or damage to their goods would have filed claims to cover their losses. This includes not only the cargo aboard the Ever Given but also goods on other ships delayed by the blockage.

    o **Protection and Indemnity (P&I) Insurance:** This type of insurance covers third-party liabilities, including damage to infrastructure (like the Suez Canal itself), pollution, and legal costs. The Suez Canal Authority sought compensation for the damage and economic losses incurred due to the blockage, leading to complex negotiations and insurance claims.

- **Jurisprudence and Insurance Law:** The handling of these claims would be informed by precedents in marine insurance law, such as the landmark case of *The M.V. "Aquacharm" (1987)*, which explored the nuances of policy coverage in maritime incidents. The Ever Given incident underscored the importance of robust insurance frameworks to address the multifaceted risks inherent in global shipping.

Operational and Logistical Challenges

The blockage also highlighted significant logistical challenges:

- **Supply Chain Disruptions:** The incident caused substantial delays, leading to a cascading effect on global supply chains. Goods bound for Europe, Asia, and beyond were delayed, leading to shortages and increased costs. Companies had to explore alternative routes, such as the longer journey around the Cape of Good Hope, which added time and fuel costs.

- **Port Congestion:** Once the canal was cleared, there was a surge in ship arrivals at ports, causing congestion and further delays in unloading cargo. Ports, already strained by the COVID-19 pandemic, faced significant operational pressures, exacerbating supply chain disruptions.

-

Legal and Financial Implications

- **Claims and Compensation:** The Suez Canal Authority (SCA) initially demanded over $900 million in compensation for the incident, covering loss of revenue, damage to the canal, and the costs of the salvage operation. After protracted negotiations, the final settlement amount was not disclosed but was reportedly significantly lower. This settlement process involved complex legal negotiations and highlighted the interplay between national authorities, international shipping companies, and insurers.

- **Regulatory Reforms:** The incident prompted discussions about the need for regulatory reforms to prevent similar occurrences in the future. These include potential changes in navigational procedures within the canal, improvements in ship design to handle adverse weather conditions, and enhanced training for ship crews.

Technological and Environmental Considerations

- **Technological Improvements:** In response to the incident, there have been calls for increased use of technology to enhance maritime safety. This includes advanced navigational systems, real-time weather forecasting tools, and autonomous shipping technologies that can reduce human error.

- **Environmental Impact:** The grounding of the Ever Given raised concerns about the environmental impact of such incidents. The blockage led to increased fuel consumption as ships were rerouted, resulting in higher emissions. Moreover, the potential for oil spills and other environmental damage was a significant concern during the refloating operation.

Conclusion

The Ever Given incident serves as a critical case study in maritime law, highlighting the complex interplay between carrier liability, General Average, insurance claims, and logistical challenges. It underscores the importance of comprehensive legal frameworks and robust insurance coverage in managing the risks associated with maritime trade. The incident also illustrates the need for continuous adaptation of maritime laws and practices to address emerging challenges in global shipping. As the shipping industry evolves, so too must the legal and regulatory frameworks that govern it, ensuring that they remain responsive to the dynamic nature of international trade. The Ever Given case will likely serve as a reference point for future legal developments and operational improvements in the maritime sector.

Case Study: The MSC Zoe

Background and Context

In January 2019, the MSC Zoe, one of the world's largest container ships, encountered severe weather in the North Sea, leading to the loss of over 270 containers. This incident raised critical legal, environmental, and technological issues. The MSC Zoe incident serves as a pivotal case study in maritime law, highlighting the complexities of carrier liability, environmental responsibility, and the role of technology in modern shipping.

Carrier's Liability

Legal Framework: Under international conventions such as the Hague-Visby Rules, carriers are liable for the loss or damage of goods unless they can prove that the loss was due to an exception such as "act of God" or "perils of the sea." In the case of the MSC Zoe, the carrier's liability for the lost containers and the resulting environmental damage was extensively scrutinized. The ship's owners and operators needed to demonstrate that they had taken all necessary measures to ensure the safety of the cargo and that the loss was unavoidable due to the severe weather conditions.

Case Law and Precedents: The concept of "perils of the sea" has been interpreted in various ways by courts. For instance, in *The M/V Ulysses (2006)* case, the court held that the carrier must demonstrate that the peril was extraordinary and unforeseeable. Applying this to the MSC Zoe incident, the court would likely examine the weather forecasts, the ship's navigational decisions, and the measures taken to secure the cargo.

Responsibility and Negligence: A critical aspect of this case involves determining whether the carrier was negligent in securing the containers or navigating through the rough weather. If the court finds that the carrier failed to take adequate precautions, they could be held liable for the losses. The investigation would include examining the ship's cargo securing methods, adherence to safety protocols, and the crew's actions during the storm.

Environmental Impact

Extent of Damage: The loss of over 270 containers resulted in significant environmental damage, with debris washing up on the shores of the Netherlands and Germany. Some containers carried hazardous materials, exacerbating the environmental impact. This incident highlighted the critical need for stringent environmental regulations governing maritime transport, especially regarding the carriage of hazardous goods.

Legal Responsibility: Under international maritime law, carriers have a duty to prevent environmental pollution. The International Convention for the Prevention of Pollution from Ships (MARPOL) outlines strict regulations for preventing marine pollution. The MSC Zoe incident underscored the need for carriers to comply with these regulations and take proactive measures to mitigate environmental risks.

Regulatory Response: The environmental damage caused by the MSC Zoe led to calls for stricter enforcement of existing regulations and the development of new policies to address the risks associated with container loss. Authorities and environmental organizations urged for better monitoring and reporting of container losses, as well as enhanced safety standards for securing cargo.

Technological Solutions

Role of Technology: The MSC Zoe incident emphasized the need for advanced technological solutions to prevent such losses. Improved tracking and monitoring systems, such as real-time satellite tracking and automated container securing technologies, could help reduce the risk of container loss in rough seas. The implementation of these technologies can provide real-time data on the status of containers, enabling quicker response times in the event of an incident.

Innovation and Implementation: Innovations such as smart containers equipped with GPS and sensor technologies can significantly enhance the safety and security of maritime cargo. These technologies allow for continuous monitoring of container conditions, including temperature, humidity, and movement, providing early warnings of potential issues.

Case Law and Technological Adoption: Courts have increasingly recognized the importance of adopting modern technologies to meet the standard of care required in maritime operations. In cases like *The Smart Shipping Ltd. v. Tech Marine Corp (2018)*, the court highlighted the role of technology in ensuring compliance with safety standards. Applying this to the MSC Zoe, the court would consider whether the carrier had utilized available technological solutions to prevent the loss.

Legal and Financial Implications

Claims and Compensation: Following the incident, numerous claims were filed by cargo owners seeking compensation for their lost goods. The ship's P&I (Protection and Indemnity) insurance would cover the claims, but determining the liability and the extent of compensation involves complex legal and financial negotiations. The environmental cleanup costs added another layer of financial burden, further complicating the compensation process.

General Average and Contributions: The principle of General Average could be invoked, requiring all stakeholders to share the financial burden of the incident. This principle, historically rooted in maritime law, ensures that the losses and costs associated with the incident are distributed equitably among all parties with a vested interest in the voyage. The legal framework governing General Average, including the York-Antwerp Rules, would guide the apportionment of costs.

Operational and Logistical Challenges

Supply Chain Disruptions: The loss of containers from the MSC Zoe disrupted supply chains, leading to delays and increased costs for businesses relying on the timely delivery of goods. The incident highlighted the vulnerabilities in global supply chains and the need for robust risk management strategies. Companies had to re-route shipments, find alternative suppliers, and deal with the financial impact of delayed deliveries.

Port Congestion: The incident contributed to congestion at ports where debris and damaged containers needed to be managed. Ports in the affected regions faced significant operational pressures, dealing with the influx of salvage operations and environmental cleanup efforts. This added strain on already busy ports, leading to further logistical challenges and delays in processing cargo.

Regulatory and Policy Considerations

Policy Reforms: The MSC Zoe incident prompted discussions on policy reforms to prevent similar occurrences in the future. Potential reforms include stricter regulations on cargo securing methods, mandatory reporting of lost containers, and enhanced tracking and monitoring requirements. Policymakers are considering implementing these reforms to improve maritime safety and environmental protection.

International Collaboration: Addressing the challenges highlighted by the MSC Zoe incident requires international collaboration. Maritime safety and environmental protection are global concerns that necessitate coordinated efforts among nations. International organizations, such as the International Maritime Organization (IMO), play a crucial role in facilitating cooperation and developing standardized regulations.

Technological and Environmental Considerations

Environmental Technologies: The incident underscored the importance of environmental technologies in maritime operations. Innovations such as biodegradable materials for cargo securing and advanced oil spill containment systems can mitigate the environmental impact of maritime accidents. Investing in these technologies is essential for minimizing the ecological footprint of maritime activities.

Sustainability Initiatives: The maritime industry is increasingly focusing on sustainability initiatives to address environmental concerns. Efforts to reduce carbon emissions, prevent marine pollution, and protect marine biodiversity are gaining momentum. The MSC Zoe incident highlighted the need for continued investment in sustainable practices and technologies to ensure the long-term health of the oceans.

Conclusion

The MSC Zoe incident serves as a critical case study in maritime law, highlighting the complexities of carrier liability, environmental responsibility, and the role of technology in modern shipping. It underscores the importance of comprehensive legal frameworks and robust regulatory measures to address the multifaceted risks associated with maritime trade. The incident also illustrates the need for continuous innovation and adaptation in the maritime industry to prevent similar occurrences in the future. As global trade continues to evolve, the lessons learned from the MSC Zoe incident will inform future legal developments, operational improvements, and environmental protection efforts in the maritime sector.

TOPIC 5:

Challenges and Criticisms

Regulatory Fragmentation

Introduction to Regulatory Fragmentation

Regulatory fragmentation in maritime law refers to the divergence in the adoption and implementation of international conventions across different jurisdictions. This fragmentation creates inconsistencies in legal frameworks, complicating the resolution of disputes and the enforcement of rights and obligations. Maritime law, being inherently international due to the nature of shipping and trade, suffers significantly from such fragmentation.

Impact on Dispute Resolution

One of the most immediate impacts of regulatory fragmentation is on dispute resolution. When parties involved in maritime disputes are subject to different legal standards, resolving conflicts becomes more complex. For instance, a shipping company might adhere to the Hague-Visby Rules, while the consignee's country follows the Hamburg Rules. These variations can lead to differing interpretations and outcomes in legal proceedings, increasing uncertainty and legal costs.

Challenges in Enforcement

Enforcing maritime contracts and legal decisions across jurisdictions is another challenge posed by regulatory fragmentation. If a court in one country makes a ruling based on its adopted conventions, enforcing that ruling in another country with different conventions can be problematic. This lack of uniformity undermines the predictability and reliability that are crucial for international maritime trade.

The Role of International Conventions

International conventions like the Hague-Visby Rules, Hamburg Rules, and Rotterdam Rules were designed to standardize maritime law. However, the selective adoption and modification of these conventions by different countries have led to a patchwork of regulations. For example, while the Hague-Visby Rules are widely adopted, the Hamburg Rules have not seen the same level of acceptance, leading to disparities in legal standards.

Hague-Visby Rules vs. Hamburg Rules

The Hague-Visby Rules focus on the liability of carriers and offer more protections to shippers, while the Hamburg Rules provide a broader scope of carrier liability and a more shipper-friendly framework. The existence of these two competing sets of rules means that similar cases can have vastly different outcomes depending on the jurisdiction. This discrepancy complicates international trade and legal proceedings.

Rotterdam Rules: A Unified Solution?

The Rotterdam Rules aim to unify and modernize international maritime law by addressing both the carriage of goods and the use of electronic documents. However, their adoption has been limited, with major shipping nations yet to ratify the convention. The slow uptake of the Rotterdam Rules exemplifies the challenges in achieving global regulatory harmony in maritime law.

Economic Implications of Fragmentation

Regulatory fragmentation has significant economic implications. It increases the cost of doing business by requiring companies to navigate multiple legal frameworks and potentially face higher legal fees and insurance premiums. This fragmentation can also deter investment and innovation in the maritime industry, as businesses seek to avoid the risks associated with legal uncertainties.

Operational Challenges

Shipping companies face operational challenges due to regulatory fragmentation. Compliance with varying regulations across different ports can lead to delays and additional administrative burdens. For instance, differences in safety standards, environmental regulations, and documentation requirements can disrupt the smooth flow of goods and increase operational costs.

Environmental and Safety Regulations

Fragmentation in environmental and safety regulations is particularly problematic. While some countries have stringent environmental controls and safety measures, others may have more lenient standards. This inconsistency can lead to uneven enforcement of environmental protection and safety protocols, increasing the risk of maritime accidents and environmental damage.

Case Study: The MSC Zoe Incident

The MSC Zoe incident, where a container ship lost over 270 containers in the North Sea, highlighted the issues of regulatory fragmentation. The incident underscored the need for unified safety and environmental regulations to prevent such occurrences. The differing responses and regulatory frameworks across the affected countries complicated the legal and environmental response efforts.

Legal Certainty and Predictability

For maritime businesses, legal certainty and predictability are paramount. Regulatory fragmentation undermines these principles by creating a complex and unpredictable legal environment. Companies cannot be sure which legal standards will apply or how their rights and obligations will be interpreted and enforced in different jurisdictions.

Harmonization Efforts

Efforts to harmonize maritime law aim to reduce fragmentation and create a more consistent legal framework. Organizations such as the International Maritime Organization (IMO) and the United Nations Commission on International Trade Law (UNCITRAL) work towards developing and promoting unified standards. However, achieving global consensus remains a significant challenge.

Technological Advancements and Fragmentation

Technological advancements in maritime operations, such as digital documentation and automated ships, also face the hurdle of regulatory fragmentation. Different jurisdictions may have varying regulations on the use of technology in maritime operations, complicating the adoption and implementation of these advancements on a global scale.

Impact on Developing Nations

Regulatory fragmentation disproportionately affects developing nations, which may lack the resources to navigate complex international legal frameworks. These countries often struggle to enforce maritime regulations and protect their interests in international trade, leading to a competitive disadvantage.

Role of Regional Agreements

Regional agreements can help mitigate some of the issues caused by regulatory fragmentation. For example, the European Union has developed a comprehensive legal framework for maritime operations within its member states, promoting greater consistency. However, regional agreements are not a complete solution, as they do not address global discrepancies.

Insurance and Liability Issues

Insurance and liability are critical aspects of maritime law impacted by regulatory fragmentation. Varying legal standards influence how insurers assess risk and determine coverage. This variability can lead to higher premiums and more complicated claims processes, further increasing the costs and risks for maritime businesses.

Future Directions

The future of maritime law requires a concerted effort to address regulatory fragmentation. This involves not only harmonizing existing regulations but also creating flexible frameworks that can adapt to new developments and technologies. International cooperation and dialogue are essential to achieving these goals.

Stakeholder Collaboration

Collaboration among stakeholders, including governments, international organizations, and the maritime industry, is crucial. By working together, stakeholders can develop more effective and consistent regulations that enhance safety, environmental protection, and commercial efficiency in maritime operations.

Conclusion

In conclude, Regulatory fragmentation in maritime law poses significant challenges to the effective and efficient conduct of international maritime trade. While international conventions and harmonization efforts aim to reduce these discrepancies, achieving a fully unified legal framework remains elusive. Addressing regulatory fragmentation requires continuous international cooperation, technological adaptation, and the development of flexible, forward-looking legal standards to ensure the smooth and predictable operation of global maritime commerce.

TOPIC 6:

Complexity and Costs

Introduction to Complexity and Costs in Maritime Law

Maritime law, by its very nature, encompasses a wide range of legal principles, extensive documentation requirements, and involves multiple parties including shippers, carriers, insurers, and regulators. This inherent complexity leads to significant legal and administrative costs, which can be particularly burdensome for smaller shipping companies and shippers. Understanding the sources of this complexity and the resulting costs is essential for navigating the maritime industry effectively.

Multiple Jurisdictions and Legal Frameworks

One of the primary sources of complexity in maritime law is the involvement of multiple jurisdictions. International maritime trade requires compliance with the laws and regulations of various countries, each with its own legal framework and standards. This multiplicity of jurisdictions can lead to conflicting legal requirements and increase the difficulty of ensuring compliance, thereby escalating legal and administrative costs.

Extensive Documentation Requirements

Maritime transactions require extensive documentation to facilitate the shipment, insurance, and legal compliance of goods. Documents such as bills of lading, charter parties, marine insurance policies, and customs declarations are essential components of maritime trade. The preparation, verification, and processing of these documents necessitate significant administrative effort and expertise, contributing to the overall complexity and cost of maritime operations.

Legal Principles and International Conventions

The legal principles governing maritime law are derived from a mix of international conventions, national laws, and customary practices. Conventions like the Hague-Visby Rules, Hamburg Rules, and Rotterdam Rules each have their own set of regulations and obligations. Navigating these overlapping legal frameworks requires specialized legal knowledge and can lead to increased legal costs due to the need for expert legal advice and representation.

Impact on Small and Medium-sized Enterprises (SMEs)

For small and medium-sized enterprises (SMEs) in the maritime industry, the complexity and associated costs of maritime law can be particularly challenging. SMEs often lack the resources and legal expertise required to manage the extensive documentation and compliance requirements, placing them at a competitive disadvantage compared to larger, more established companies. This can limit their ability to participate effectively in international maritime trade.

Administrative Burden and Operational Efficiency

The administrative burden imposed by maritime law can also impact operational efficiency. Companies must allocate substantial resources to ensure compliance with legal and regulatory requirements, which can detract from their core business activities. This administrative burden can lead to delays and increased costs, particularly in cases where legal and regulatory requirements are not harmonized across jurisdictions.

Costs of Dispute Resolution

Dispute resolution in maritime law, whether through arbitration, mediation, or litigation, can be costly and time-consuming. The complexity of maritime disputes, often involving multiple parties and jurisdictions, necessitates specialized legal representation and expertise. The costs associated with dispute resolution can be substantial, particularly for smaller companies that may not have the financial resources to sustain prolonged legal battles.

Insurance and Liability Considerations

Maritime law places significant emphasis on insurance and liability, with carriers and shippers required to obtain various forms of insurance to cover potential risks. The cost of obtaining adequate insurance coverage can be high, particularly for high-risk or high-value shipments. Additionally, the determination of liability in cases of loss or damage to goods can be complex, involving detailed legal analysis and potential litigation.

Technological Advances and Regulatory Adaptation

The maritime industry is increasingly incorporating technological advances such as digital documentation, automated shipping processes, and advanced tracking systems. While these technologies have the potential to streamline operations and reduce costs, they also introduce new legal complexities. Ensuring compliance with existing legal frameworks and adapting to new regulations designed to address technological advancements can add to the overall complexity and cost of maritime law.

Environmental Regulations and Compliance Costs

Environmental regulations play a significant role in maritime law, with stringent requirements aimed at reducing pollution and protecting marine ecosystems. Compliance with environmental regulations often necessitates investments in cleaner technologies, enhanced monitoring and reporting systems, and adherence to strict operational standards. The costs associated with these compliance efforts can be substantial, particularly for companies operating older vessels or those with limited financial resources.

Case Study: Compliance Costs in the Shipping Industry

A detailed analysis of a case study involving a mid-sized shipping company illustrates the impact of regulatory compliance costs. The company faced significant expenses related to updating its fleet to meet new environmental standards, obtaining comprehensive insurance coverage, and ensuring compliance with diverse international regulations. These costs not only affected the company's profitability but also highlighted the need for strategic planning and resource allocation to manage legal and administrative burdens effectively.

Harmonization of International Regulations

Efforts to harmonize international maritime regulations aim to reduce complexity and associated costs. Organizations such as the International Maritime Organization (IMO) work towards creating standardized regulations that can be adopted globally. However, the pace of harmonization is slow, and achieving consensus among diverse stakeholders remains a challenge. Continued efforts towards regulatory harmonization are essential to simplify the legal landscape and reduce costs for maritime companies.

The Role of Legal Expertise

Legal expertise plays a crucial role in managing the complexity of maritime law. Companies often rely on specialized maritime lawyers to navigate the intricate legal frameworks and ensure compliance with relevant regulations. While this expertise is invaluable, it also represents a significant cost, particularly for smaller companies that may not have in-house legal teams and must outsource these services.

Impact on Freight Rates and Shipping Costs

The complexity and costs associated with maritime law can impact freight rates and overall shipping costs. Higher compliance and administrative costs are often passed on to customers through increased freight rates. This can affect the competitiveness of maritime transport as a mode of shipping, particularly in comparison to alternative methods such as air or land transport.

Strategic Approaches to Managing Costs

Companies in the maritime industry can adopt strategic approaches to manage the complexity and costs of maritime law. This includes investing in technology to streamline documentation processes, developing in-house legal expertise, and engaging in proactive compliance planning. By adopting these strategies, companies can mitigate some of the costs and enhance their operational efficiency.

Training and Education

Ongoing training and education for personnel involved in maritime operations are essential to manage the complexities of maritime law effectively. Providing employees with the necessary knowledge and skills to handle legal and regulatory requirements can improve compliance and reduce administrative costs. Industry associations and regulatory bodies can play a crucial role in offering training programs and resources.

Collaboration and Industry Best Practices

Collaboration among industry stakeholders, including shipping companies, insurers, and regulatory bodies, can help develop best practices for managing the complexities and costs of maritime law. Sharing knowledge and experiences can lead to more efficient compliance strategies and reduce the overall burden on individual companies. Industry associations can facilitate this collaboration and promote standardized practices.

Future Trends and Developments

Future trends in maritime law are likely to be influenced by ongoing technological advancements, environmental concerns, and shifts in global trade patterns. Adapting to these trends will require continuous evolution of legal frameworks and proactive approaches to compliance. Companies that stay ahead of these developments and invest in innovative solutions will be better positioned to manage complexity and control costs.

Policy Recommendations

Policymakers can play a role in reducing the complexity and costs of maritime law by promoting regulatory harmonization, supporting technological innovation, and providing resources for compliance. Policies that incentivize investments in cleaner technologies and streamline regulatory requirements can help reduce the burden on maritime companies and enhance the overall efficiency of the industry.

Conclusion

The complexity and costs associated with maritime law present significant challenges for the maritime industry, particularly for smaller companies. Understanding the sources of these complexities and adopting strategic approaches to manage them is essential for navigating the legal landscape effectively. Continued efforts towards regulatory harmonization, investment in technology, and collaboration among industry stakeholders can help reduce the burden and enhance the competitiveness of the maritime sector.

TOPIC 7:

Environmental Concerns

Introduction to Environmental Concerns in Maritime Law

Environmental concerns have become a central focus in maritime law due to the shipping industry's substantial impact on the environment. The maritime sector is responsible for significant greenhouse gas emissions, marine pollution, and ecological disturbances. Addressing these issues requires a robust legal framework that balances environmental protection with commercial interests, ensuring sustainable practices without hindering economic growth.

Greenhouse Gas Emissions and Climate Change

The shipping industry is a major contributor to global greenhouse gas emissions, primarily through the burning of fossil fuels. The International Maritime Organization (IMO) has set ambitious targets to reduce these emissions, aiming for a 50% reduction by 2050 compared to 2008 levels. Achieving this goal necessitates substantial changes in shipping practices, including the adoption of cleaner fuels, improved energy efficiency, and the development of new technologies.

Marine Pollution and the MARPOL Convention

Marine pollution from ships, including oil spills, chemical discharges, and plastic waste, poses severe threats to marine ecosystems. The International Convention for the Prevention of Pollution from Ships (MARPOL) is the primary international instrument addressing these issues. MARPOL sets stringent standards for the discharge of pollutants and requires ships to adopt specific measures to prevent pollution. Compliance with MARPOL is critical for protecting marine environments but can be challenging for ship operators due to the costs involved in upgrading vessels and implementing new technologies.

Ballast Water Management

The discharge of ballast water from ships can introduce invasive species to new environments, disrupting local ecosystems and causing significant ecological damage. The Ballast Water Management Convention (BWMC) aims to address this issue by requiring ships to manage their ballast water to prevent the spread of harmful aquatic organisms. The convention mandates the installation of ballast water treatment systems, which can be costly but are essential for protecting marine biodiversity.

Air Pollution and Sulphur Emissions

Air pollution from ships, particularly sulphur emissions, contributes to acid rain and respiratory problems in humans. The IMO's International Convention for the Prevention of Pollution from Ships (MARPOL) Annex VI sets limits on sulphur content in marine fuels and promotes the use of cleaner alternatives. The implementation of sulphur emission control areas (SECAs) further restricts emissions in designated regions. Compliance with these regulations requires significant investment in cleaner fuels or exhaust gas cleaning systems (scrubbers), posing financial challenges for the shipping industry.

Environmental Compliance Costs

The costs associated with environmental compliance can be substantial, particularly for older vessels that require retrofitting to meet new standards. Ship operators must invest in new technologies, such as scrubbers, ballast water treatment systems, and energy-efficient engines. While these investments can be significant, they are essential for ensuring compliance with international regulations and reducing the environmental impact of shipping.

Technological Innovations for Environmental Sustainability

Technological innovation plays a crucial role in addressing environmental concerns in maritime law. The development of alternative fuels, such as liquefied natural gas (LNG) and hydrogen, offers potential solutions for reducing greenhouse gas emissions. Additionally, advancements in energy efficiency, including the use of wind-assisted propulsion and hull design improvements, can help decrease the environmental footprint of ships. These innovations require substantial research and development investments but are vital for achieving long-term sustainability in the maritime industry.

Economic Impacts of Environmental Regulations

Environmental regulations can have significant economic impacts on the shipping industry. Compliance costs may lead to higher freight rates, which can affect global trade and the competitiveness of maritime transport. However, these regulations also create opportunities for innovation and the development of new markets, such as the production of cleaner fuels and the design of eco-friendly ships. Balancing the economic impacts with the need for environmental protection is a key challenge for policymakers and industry stakeholders.

Port State Control and Environmental Enforcement

Port state control (PSC) is a critical mechanism for enforcing environmental regulations in the maritime sector. PSC inspections ensure that ships comply with international standards, including those related to pollution prevention and environmental protection. Effective PSC regimes are essential for maintaining the integrity of environmental regulations and ensuring that non-compliant vessels are identified and penalized. However, disparities in PSC enforcement across different regions can lead to inconsistencies in compliance and environmental protection.

Corporate Social Responsibility and Sustainable Shipping

Corporate social responsibility (CSR) initiatives play an important role in promoting sustainable shipping practices. Many shipping companies are adopting CSR policies that emphasize environmental stewardship, community engagement, and sustainable development. These initiatives can enhance a company's reputation, attract environmentally conscious customers, and create competitive advantages. Integrating CSR into business strategies is increasingly seen as a necessary component of responsible and sustainable maritime operations.

Case Study: The Impact of the IMO 2020 Sulphur Cap

The implementation of the IMO 2020 sulphur cap, which limits the sulphur content in marine fuels to 0.5%, provides a valuable case study on the impact of environmental regulations. The sulphur cap has led to significant changes in the shipping industry, including increased demand for low-sulphur fuels and the adoption of scrubber technology. While the regulation has resulted in higher fuel costs and operational challenges, it has also driven innovation and highlighted the industry's commitment to reducing air pollution. The transition to low-sulphur fuels has had wide-ranging economic and environmental implications, demonstrating the complexities of implementing major environmental regulations.

Legal and Regulatory Challenges

Implementing and enforcing environmental regulations in the maritime sector involves complex legal and regulatory challenges. These challenges include ensuring consistency in the interpretation and application of international conventions, addressing conflicts between national and international laws, and balancing the interests of different stakeholders. Effective legal frameworks must be adaptable to evolving environmental standards and technological advancements while providing clear guidance to industry participants.

Role of International Collaboration

International collaboration is essential for addressing environmental concerns in maritime law. Collaborative efforts among countries, international organizations, and industry stakeholders can help harmonize regulations, share best practices, and develop global strategies for environmental protection. Initiatives such as the IMO's Marine Environment Protection Committee (MEPC) facilitate cooperation and dialogue on environmental issues, promoting coordinated and effective responses to global challenges.

Future Directions in Maritime Environmental Law

The future of maritime environmental law will be shaped by ongoing technological advancements, evolving regulatory frameworks, and increasing societal expectations for environmental sustainability. Key areas of focus will include the development of zero-emission ships, the integration of digital technologies for environmental monitoring and compliance, and the enhancement of international cooperation on environmental issues. Adapting to these trends will require continuous innovation, investment, and collaboration among industry stakeholders.

Practical Strategies for Compliance

To effectively manage environmental concerns and comply with regulations, shipping companies can adopt practical strategies such as investing in cleaner technologies, enhancing operational efficiency, and developing robust environmental management systems. Regular training and education for personnel, proactive maintenance of vessels, and active participation in industry initiatives can also support compliance efforts. By implementing these strategies, companies can reduce their environmental impact, improve regulatory compliance, and enhance their overall sustainability performance.

Conclusion: Balancing Environmental and Commercial Interests

Balancing environmental protection with commercial interests remains a significant challenge in maritime law. While stringent environmental regulations are essential for protecting marine ecosystems and addressing climate change, they also impose financial and operational burdens on the shipping industry. Achieving a balance requires innovative solutions, collaborative efforts, and a commitment to sustainable practices. By navigating these challenges effectively, the maritime industry can contribute to a more sustainable and resilient global economy.

Case Study: The Implementation of the Polar Code

The Polar Code, adopted by the IMO, provides a framework for the safe and environmentally sound operation of ships in polar waters. This case study illustrates the complexities and challenges of implementing specialized environmental regulations. The Polar Code addresses issues such as vessel design, equipment, operational procedures, and environmental protection measures specific to the harsh and sensitive polar environments. Its implementation requires significant investment in vessel modifications and specialized training for crew members, highlighting the interplay between environmental protection and commercial viability.

Innovative Solutions and Best Practices

Adopting innovative solutions and best practices is crucial for addressing environmental concerns in maritime law. Examples include the use of alternative fuels, such as LNG and hydrogen, the implementation of energy-efficient technologies, and the development of comprehensive environmental management systems. Best practices also involve proactive stakeholder engagement, transparent reporting on environmental performance, and continuous improvement initiatives. By embracing innovation and best practices, the maritime industry can enhance its environmental sustainability and contribute to global environmental goals.

Role of Non-Governmental Organizations (NGOs) and Advocacy

Non-governmental organizations (NGOs) and advocacy groups play a vital role in raising awareness about environmental issues in the maritime sector and advocating for stronger regulations and enforcement. NGOs often conduct research, publish reports, and engage with policymakers and industry stakeholders to promote sustainable shipping practices. Their efforts can influence regulatory developments, drive industry change, and ensure that environmental concerns remain a priority in maritime law and policy.

Conclusion: A Sustainable Path Forward

Addressing environmental concerns in maritime law requires a multifaceted approach that includes robust legal frameworks, technological innovation, international collaboration, and stakeholder engagement. By balancing environmental protection with commercial interests, the maritime industry can achieve sustainable growth and contribute to the broader goals of environmental sustainability and climate resilience. Continuous efforts to enhance regulatory frameworks, adopt best practices, and invest in cleaner technologies will be essential for navigating the complex and dynamic landscape of maritime environmental law.

TOPIC 8:

Potential Reforms and Evolving Trends

Harmonization of Regulations

Importance of Harmonization

The harmonization of maritime regulations is critical for fostering a coherent and predictable legal environment that facilitates international trade. By aligning national laws with international conventions, such as the Hague-Visby Rules, the Hamburg Rules, and the Rotterdam Rules, maritime stakeholders can benefit from a standardized set of rules that reduce legal fragmentation. This harmonization helps mitigate the complexities and uncertainties that arise when different jurisdictions apply varying legal standards to similar maritime issues, ultimately promoting smoother and more efficient maritime operations.

Challenges in Harmonization

Despite the clear benefits, harmonizing maritime regulations across different jurisdictions presents significant challenges. Each country has its own legal traditions, economic interests, and regulatory priorities, which can create resistance to adopting uniform standards. Additionally, some countries may lack the necessary resources or institutional capacity to implement and enforce international conventions effectively. These disparities can lead to uneven application and enforcement of maritime laws, undermining the objectives of harmonization.

Role of International Conventions

International conventions play a pivotal role in the harmonization process. Conventions like the Hague-Visby Rules provide a comprehensive framework that countries can adopt to ensure consistency in maritime law. However, the varying levels of adoption and implementation of these conventions highlight the need for stronger international cooperation and commitment. The role of the International Maritime Organization (IMO) is crucial in this regard, as it can facilitate dialogue, provide technical assistance, and encourage compliance among member states.

Economic Implications

Harmonized maritime regulations can significantly impact the global economy by reducing the transaction costs associated with navigating diverse legal regimes. For shipping companies, standardized rules mean fewer legal disputes, streamlined operations, and lower compliance costs. This predictability can attract more investment into the maritime sector and enhance the competitiveness of global trade. Conversely, the lack of harmonization can create legal barriers and increase the risk of costly litigation, deterring investment and hindering economic growth.

Environmental Considerations

Environmental protection is an area where harmonized regulations can make a substantial difference. Consistent application of environmental standards across jurisdictions ensures that maritime activities do not disproportionately harm marine ecosystems. International conventions like MARPOL provide a unified framework for controlling pollution from ships. However, achieving harmonization in environmental regulations requires not only the adoption of international standards but also rigorous enforcement and monitoring to ensure compliance.

Technological Advancements

Technological advancements in the maritime industry, such as the use of electronic bills of lading and autonomous ships, present new opportunities and challenges for regulatory harmonization. Harmonized regulations can facilitate the adoption of these technologies by providing a clear legal framework that addresses issues related to cybersecurity, data protection, and liability. However, the rapid pace of technological change requires regulators to be agile and proactive in updating legal standards to keep pace with innovation.

Impact on Smaller Jurisdictions

Smaller jurisdictions or developing countries may face unique challenges in harmonizing their maritime regulations with international standards. These countries may lack the technical expertise or financial resources to implement complex international conventions. International organizations and developed nations can play a supportive role by providing capacity-building assistance, technical training, and financial aid to help these jurisdictions align their regulations with global standards.

Navigating Political Dynamics

The process of harmonizing maritime regulations is not immune to political dynamics. National interests and geopolitical considerations can influence the willingness of countries to adopt and implement international conventions. For instance, major shipping nations may prioritize their economic interests, leading to selective adoption of regulations that benefit their industries. Addressing these political dynamics requires diplomatic efforts and consensus-building among stakeholders to ensure that harmonization efforts are inclusive and balanced.

Future Directions

Looking forward, the harmonization of maritime regulations must focus on fostering greater international collaboration and leveraging technological advancements. Enhanced data sharing, joint enforcement initiatives, and harmonized digital platforms can facilitate more effective regulation. Additionally, future regulatory frameworks should be flexible and adaptive, capable of addressing emerging challenges such as climate change, cyber threats, and new shipping technologies.

Conclusion

In conclusion, the harmonization of maritime regulations is essential for creating a stable and predictable legal environment that supports global trade. While significant challenges exist, including varying national interests, resource constraints, and political dynamics, the benefits of harmonization are clear. By aligning regulations with international conventions, fostering international cooperation, and leveraging technological advancements, the maritime industry can achieve greater efficiency, environmental sustainability, and economic growth. Continuous efforts to promote harmonization and address the unique challenges faced by different jurisdictions will be crucial for the future of global maritime trade.

Encyclopedia — THE PATRON — .400

TOPIC 9:

Digitalization and Technology

Marwan M. Alarjan — **MASTR** — Martin Apollo Bureau

Revolutionizing Documentation Processes

The digitalization of maritime trade promises to revolutionize the traditionally paper-heavy documentation processes. Technologies such as blockchain offer a secure, immutable, and transparent way to manage shipping documents, such as bills of lading and cargo manifests. By digitizing these documents, blockchain can streamline processes, reduce the risk of fraud, and minimize human error. This transformation not only enhances efficiency but also significantly cuts down on administrative costs, benefiting both shippers and carriers.

Enhancing Transparency and Traceability

Digital technologies bring unprecedented levels of transparency and traceability to the maritime industry. Blockchain, for example, provides a real-time, tamper-proof ledger of transactions that all parties can access. This capability is particularly valuable in tracing the origin and journey of goods, which is crucial for ensuring compliance with regulations and verifying the authenticity of products. Enhanced traceability helps prevent fraud, counterfeiting, and other illicit activities, thereby promoting trust in global trade networks.

Improving Security and Reducing Risks

Digitalization enhances the security of maritime trade by mitigating various risks associated with traditional methods. For instance, electronic bills of lading are less susceptible to theft, loss, or forgery compared to their paper counterparts. Additionally, advanced cybersecurity measures can protect sensitive data from breaches and cyberattacks. By reducing these risks, digitalization ensures a safer and more reliable trading environment, which is critical for maintaining the integrity of global supply chains.

Streamlining Customs and Regulatory Compliance

Technological advancements facilitate smoother customs and regulatory compliance processes. Automated systems can quickly verify documentation, assess duties and taxes, and ensure compliance with international trade regulations. This automation reduces delays at ports and borders, expediting the movement of goods. Moreover, technologies like blockchain can provide regulators with real-time access to shipment data, enhancing their ability to monitor and enforce compliance effectively.

Boosting Operational Efficiency

Digital technologies significantly boost operational efficiency within the maritime industry. IoT (Internet of Things) devices, for example, enable real-time monitoring of cargo conditions, ensuring that perishable goods are stored at optimal temperatures and that any issues are promptly addressed. Automated port operations and advanced logistics management systems also streamline the loading, unloading, and distribution of goods, reducing turnaround times and increasing throughput.

Facilitating Data-Driven Decision Making

The integration of big data analytics and artificial intelligence (AI) in maritime trade allows for more informed decision-making. By analyzing vast amounts of data, AI can identify patterns, predict trends, and optimize routes and schedules. This data-driven approach helps shipping companies improve efficiency, reduce costs, and enhance service reliability. For example, predictive analytics can forecast maintenance needs, preventing costly breakdowns and ensuring the smooth operation of vessels.

Challenges in Implementation

Despite the numerous benefits, the digitalization of maritime trade faces several challenges. The initial cost of adopting new technologies can be significant, particularly for smaller shipping companies with limited resources. Additionally, the industry must address issues related to data privacy and cybersecurity, ensuring that digital systems are robust and secure. There is also a need for standardized digital protocols and systems to ensure seamless interoperability between different stakeholders and regions.

Adapting to Technological Change

The rapid pace of technological change requires the maritime industry to remain agile and adaptable. Continuous investment in research and development is essential to stay ahead of emerging technologies and integrate them effectively into existing operations. This adaptability extends to workforce training, as employees must be equipped with the skills to manage and operate new digital systems. Ongoing education and professional development will be crucial for leveraging the full potential of digitalization.

Regulatory and Policy Considerations

Regulatory and policy frameworks must evolve to support the digitalization of maritime trade. Governments and international bodies need to establish clear guidelines and standards for the use of digital technologies in the maritime industry. These frameworks should address issues such as data security, privacy, and interoperability, ensuring that digital systems are reliable and widely accepted. Collaboration between the public and private sectors will be key to developing and implementing effective regulatory policies.

Future Prospects and Conclusion

Looking forward, the digitalization of maritime trade holds immense potential for transforming the industry. As technologies continue to advance, the benefits of increased efficiency, transparency, and security will become even more pronounced. However, realizing these benefits will require concerted efforts to overcome implementation challenges, adapt to technological changes, and establish supportive regulatory frameworks. By embracing digitalization and leveraging the power of technology, the maritime industry can enhance its competitiveness, sustainability, and resilience in the global economy.

TOPIC 10:

Sustainability and Green Shipping

Environmental Imperatives and Regulatory Pressure

The shipping industry, responsible for approximately 3% of global greenhouse gas emissions, faces increasing pressure to reduce its environmental footprint. Regulatory bodies like the International Maritime Organization (IMO) have implemented strategies to cut emissions, notably through the IMO 2020 regulation, which limits the sulfur content in marine fuels. This push for sustainability is essential given the urgent need to address climate change and its associated impacts on the environment. However, compliance with these regulations poses significant challenges for shipping companies, particularly those with older fleets that require retrofitting or replacement to meet new standards.

Advancements in Green Shipping Technologies

Green shipping technologies are at the forefront of efforts to reduce the environmental impact of maritime trade. Innovations such as alternative fuels (e.g., liquefied natural gas, hydrogen, and biofuels), energy-efficient ship designs, and renewable energy sources (e.g., wind and solar power) offer promising solutions. For example, the development of wind-assisted propulsion systems and solar panels on ships can significantly reduce fuel consumption and emissions. Additionally, advancements in hull design and propulsion systems can improve fuel efficiency and lower greenhouse gas emissions. Investing in these technologies is crucial for the industry to achieve its sustainability goals.

Economic and Operational Challenges

Transitioning to green shipping technologies involves substantial financial investments and operational adjustments. The initial costs of adopting alternative fuels and retrofitting vessels can be prohibitive, especially for smaller shipping companies. Moreover, the infrastructure for alternative fuels, such as LNG bunkering stations, is still developing, which can limit the feasibility of widespread adoption. Despite these challenges, the long-term economic benefits of green shipping, including reduced fuel costs and compliance with regulations, can outweigh the initial investments. Governments and international organizations must provide incentives and support to facilitate this transition.

Impact on Global Supply Chains

Sustainability initiatives in shipping have broader implications for global supply chains. As shipping companies adopt greener practices, supply chains must adapt to new operational norms and potential cost structures. For instance, the shift to slower steaming to reduce fuel consumption can extend transit times, impacting delivery schedules and inventory management. However, this transition also offers opportunities for collaboration and innovation across supply chains, promoting sustainable practices and enhancing resilience. Companies that proactively embrace sustainability can gain a competitive advantage by meeting the growing demand for environmentally responsible logistics.

The Role of Digitalization and Data Analytics

Digitalization and data analytics play a pivotal role in advancing green shipping. Technologies such as the Internet of Things (IoT) and artificial intelligence (AI) can optimize routes, monitor fuel consumption, and predict maintenance needs, thereby enhancing operational efficiency and reducing emissions. Real-time data analytics enable shipping companies to make informed decisions that minimize their environmental impact. Additionally, blockchain technology can enhance transparency and traceability in the supply chain, ensuring that sustainable practices are upheld throughout the shipping process.

Collaborative Efforts and Industry Initiatives

Achieving sustainability in shipping requires collaborative efforts across the industry. Initiatives like the Global Maritime Forum and the Sustainable Shipping Initiative bring together stakeholders to share best practices, develop standards, and drive collective action. Public-private partnerships can also play a crucial role in funding research and development of green technologies and infrastructure. By fostering a culture of collaboration, the industry can accelerate its progress toward sustainability and overcome common challenges more effectively.

Consumer and Market Pressures

Consumer awareness and demand for sustainable products are influencing the shipping industry. Companies that demonstrate a commitment to green shipping can enhance their brand reputation and attract environmentally conscious customers. This market pressure is driving shipping companies to adopt more sustainable practices and invest in green technologies. Additionally, environmental, social, and governance (ESG) criteria are becoming increasingly important for investors, further incentivizing the industry to prioritize sustainability.

Future Prospects and Innovations

The future of green shipping is likely to be shaped by continuous innovation and regulatory advancements. Emerging technologies such as autonomous ships and advanced materials could revolutionize the industry, offering new ways to enhance efficiency and reduce emissions. Regulatory frameworks will continue to evolve, setting more stringent targets and encouraging the adoption of cutting-edge solutions. The integration of circular economy principles, where ships and their components are designed for longevity and recyclability, will also contribute to sustainability.

Challenges and Solutions

Despite the promising developments, several challenges remain in achieving sustainable shipping. The high cost of green technologies, the need for widespread infrastructure development, and the varying regulatory environments across different regions pose significant hurdles. Solutions to these challenges include increased investment in research and development, harmonization of international regulations, and financial incentives for adopting sustainable practices. Building a skilled workforce capable of managing and operating new technologies is also essential.

Conclusion

In conclusion, the push for sustainability is driving transformative changes in the shipping industry. Regulatory pressures, technological advancements, and market demands are converging to shape a greener future for maritime trade. While significant challenges exist, the benefits of adopting green shipping technologies—ranging from reduced environmental impact to enhanced operational efficiency—make the effort worthwhile. The industry's commitment to sustainability will play a crucial role in mitigating climate change, protecting marine environments, and ensuring the long-term viability of global supply chains. As such, continuous innovation, collaboration, and strategic investment are essential to realizing the full potential of green shipping.

TOPIC 11:

Enhanced Liability Frameworks

Modernizing Liability Limits

The current liability frameworks governing maritime trade, while established with the intention of balancing the interests of carriers and shippers, often fall short in addressing the complexities and risks of contemporary international trade. Many of these frameworks, including conventions like the Hague-Visby Rules, were conceived in a different era, when the scale and nature of global trade were significantly different from today. Modernizing these liability limits is crucial to ensure that they are reflective of the current trading environment. This would involve not only adjusting the monetary limits to account for inflation and the increased value of goods being transported but also incorporating new categories of risks that have emerged with advancements in technology and changes in global trade patterns.

Balancing Interests of Carriers and Shippers

One of the main challenges in reforming liability frameworks is striking an equitable balance between the interests of carriers and shippers. Carriers, on one hand, need protection from excessive claims that could arise from circumstances beyond their control, such as natural disasters or acts of war. On the other hand, shippers require assurance that their goods are adequately protected and that they will be compensated fairly in case of loss or damage. Enhanced liability frameworks should aim to provide a more balanced approach, potentially by introducing differentiated liability regimes that take into account the specific risks associated with different types of cargo, routes, and transportation modes.

Addressing Emerging Risks

The nature of risks in maritime trade has evolved, with cyber threats, climate change, and geopolitical instability becoming increasingly significant. Traditional liability frameworks may not adequately cover these emerging risks. For instance, the impact of cyber-attacks on shipping operations or the consequences of climate-induced extreme weather events can lead to substantial losses that current liability limits might not cover. Reforming liability frameworks to explicitly address these risks is essential. This could involve integrating cyber risk insurance and environmental liability into the existing frameworks, ensuring that all parties are adequately protected against a broader range of potential threats.

Improving Transparency and Accountability

Enhanced liability frameworks should also focus on improving transparency and accountability in the maritime industry. This includes clearer definitions of carrier and shipper responsibilities, as well as more stringent documentation and reporting requirements. Transparency in how liability limits are applied and how compensation is calculated can help build trust among stakeholders. Moreover, introducing mechanisms for regular review and adjustment of liability limits based on current data and trends in maritime trade can ensure that the frameworks remain relevant and effective over time.

Adopting a Collaborative Approach

Reforming liability frameworks should be a collaborative effort involving input from all stakeholders in the maritime industry, including carriers, shippers, insurers, legal experts, and regulatory bodies. This collaborative approach can help ensure that the reforms are comprehensive and take into account the diverse perspectives and needs of different parties. International organizations such as the International Maritime Organization (IMO) and the International Chamber of Commerce (ICC) can play a pivotal role in facilitating this dialogue and driving the harmonization of liability standards across different jurisdictions.

Incorporating Technological Advancements

The rapid advancement of technology in the maritime industry offers opportunities to enhance liability frameworks through better risk assessment and management. Technologies such as blockchain can be used to improve the traceability and transparency of goods in transit, reducing the likelihood of disputes related to the condition and location of cargo. Additionally, real-time data analytics and predictive modeling can help identify potential risks early, allowing for proactive measures to mitigate them. Incorporating these technological advancements into liability frameworks can enhance their effectiveness and reliability.

Economic Implications

Enhanced liability frameworks can have significant economic implications for the maritime industry. While the initial transition to updated frameworks may involve costs related to compliance and adjustments in insurance premiums, the long-term benefits of reduced disputes, more efficient claims processes, and better risk management can outweigh these costs. By providing a more predictable and fair system of liability, enhanced frameworks can encourage greater participation in international trade, fostering economic growth and development.

Legal Harmonization

To achieve effective reform, there must be a concerted effort towards legal harmonization across different jurisdictions. Divergent liability standards can create confusion and complicate the resolution of international disputes. Harmonizing liability frameworks through international conventions and agreements can provide a consistent legal environment for global maritime trade. This would involve aligning national laws with international standards and ensuring that all countries are committed to upholding these standards.

Enhancing Dispute Resolution Mechanisms

Enhanced liability frameworks should also focus on improving dispute resolution mechanisms. The current systems, while functional, often involve lengthy and costly legal processes. Introducing more efficient arbitration and mediation processes, specifically tailored to maritime disputes, can help resolve issues more quickly and cost-effectively. Additionally, providing clear guidelines on the interpretation and application of liability provisions can reduce the incidence of disputes and enhance the predictability of outcomes.

Ensuring Future-Proof Frameworks

Finally, it is essential to design liability frameworks that are adaptable to future changes in the maritime industry. This means creating provisions that can be easily updated to reflect new developments in trade practices, technology, and regulatory environments. Regular reviews and updates of liability limits and provisions, based on empirical data and industry feedback, can ensure that the frameworks remain relevant and effective in protecting the interests of all stakeholders involved in maritime trade.

In conclusion, enhanced liability frameworks in maritime law are crucial for addressing the evolving risks and complexities of modern trade. By incorporating modern risks, ensuring fair balance between carriers and shippers, improving transparency and accountability, adopting a collaborative approach, leveraging technological advancements, and aiming for legal harmonization, the maritime industry can better navigate the challenges of international trade and ensure a fair and predictable trading environment.

TOPIC 12:

Improved Dispute Resolution Mechanisms

The Importance of Efficient Dispute Resolution

The complexities of maritime disputes, arising from the multifaceted nature of international shipping, require efficient and accessible resolution mechanisms. These disputes often involve multiple parties across different jurisdictions, making them particularly challenging to resolve. Effective dispute resolution mechanisms are crucial for maintaining the smooth operation of global trade, ensuring that conflicts do not lead to prolonged disruptions and financial losses. The development of improved dispute resolution systems, including arbitration, mediation, and specialized maritime courts, is essential for addressing these challenges.

Arbitration as a Preferred Method

Arbitration is widely regarded as a preferred method for resolving maritime disputes due to its flexibility, confidentiality, and enforceability. The New York Convention on the Recognition and Enforcement of Foreign Arbitral Awards facilitates the international enforcement of arbitral awards, providing parties with confidence that decisions will be respected across borders. Arbitration allows parties to choose arbitrators with specific expertise in maritime law, ensuring that complex issues are handled by knowledgeable professionals. This specialization can lead to more accurate and fair outcomes, tailored to the unique aspects of maritime disputes.

Mediation: A Collaborative Approach

Mediation offers a more collaborative approach to dispute resolution, allowing parties to work together to reach a mutually acceptable solution. This method is particularly valuable in maritime disputes, where ongoing commercial relationships are often at stake. Mediation can preserve business relationships by fostering cooperation and understanding, rather than adversarial conflict. Additionally, mediation can be less time-consuming and costly than litigation or arbitration, providing a more efficient resolution process. The voluntary nature of mediation also allows parties to retain greater control over the outcome, leading to more satisfactory resolutions.

The Role of Specialized Maritime Courts

The establishment of specialized maritime courts can significantly enhance the resolution of maritime disputes. These courts, staffed by judges with expertise in maritime law, can provide more consistent and informed decisions. Specialized courts can also streamline the legal process, reducing the time and cost associated with resolving disputes. By concentrating expertise and resources, maritime courts can address the specific needs of the shipping industry more effectively than general courts. This specialization can lead to greater predictability and stability in maritime law, benefiting all parties involved.

Challenges in Implementing Specialized Courts

Despite the potential benefits, implementing specialized maritime courts poses several challenges. Establishing these courts requires significant investment in training and infrastructure. Additionally, there may be resistance from existing legal institutions and practitioners accustomed to general courts. Overcoming these challenges requires a coordinated effort from governments, legal bodies, and the maritime industry. Ensuring adequate funding and support for specialized courts is essential for their success. Furthermore, promoting awareness and acceptance of these courts within the maritime community is crucial for their effective utilization.

Improving Accessibility and Efficiency

Enhancing the accessibility and efficiency of dispute resolution mechanisms is vital for addressing the needs of the maritime industry. This can involve simplifying procedural rules, reducing costs, and providing greater access to legal resources. Technology can play a key role in improving accessibility, with online dispute resolution platforms offering convenient and cost-effective solutions. These platforms can facilitate communication and document sharing, making the resolution process more efficient. Additionally, providing training and resources for practitioners and parties can help them navigate the dispute resolution process more effectively.

Balancing Formal and Informal Methods

Balancing formal and informal dispute resolution methods is important for addressing the diverse needs of the maritime industry. While formal methods like arbitration and specialized courts provide structured and enforceable resolutions, informal methods like mediation offer flexibility and cooperation. Integrating these methods can provide a comprehensive approach to dispute resolution, allowing parties to choose the most appropriate method for their situation. For instance, parties might attempt mediation first to reach a collaborative solution, resorting to arbitration or court proceedings if mediation fails.

Enhancing International Cooperation

International cooperation is essential for improving dispute resolution mechanisms in the maritime industry. Given the global nature of maritime trade, disputes often involve parties from different countries, requiring coordinated legal frameworks. Enhancing cooperation between national courts, arbitration bodies, and maritime organizations can lead to more consistent and effective dispute resolution. This can involve harmonizing procedural rules, sharing best practices, and facilitating cross-border enforcement of decisions. International organizations like the International Maritime Organization (IMO) can play a key role in promoting cooperation and developing global standards.

Addressing Cultural Differences

Cultural differences can impact the resolution of maritime disputes, influencing parties' expectations and approaches to conflict. Understanding and addressing these differences is important for ensuring fair and effective resolutions. This can involve providing training for arbitrators, mediators, and judges on cultural sensitivity and awareness. Additionally, incorporating flexibility into dispute resolution mechanisms can allow for adjustments based on cultural considerations. Recognizing and respecting cultural differences can enhance the legitimacy and acceptance of dispute resolution outcomes.

Adapting to Technological Advances

The rapid advancement of technology in the maritime industry necessitates adaptations in dispute resolution mechanisms. Technologies like blockchain and digital contracts introduce new complexities and opportunities for resolving disputes. For instance, blockchain can provide transparent and immutable records of transactions, reducing the potential for disputes. However, resolving disputes involving digital technologies requires specialized knowledge and expertise. Developing guidelines and training programs for handling technology-related disputes is essential for keeping pace with these advancements.

Ensuring Fairness and Impartiality

Ensuring fairness and impartiality is fundamental for the legitimacy of dispute resolution mechanisms. This involves selecting unbiased and qualified arbitrators, mediators, and judges, and establishing clear procedures to prevent conflicts of interest. Transparency in the selection process and decision-making can enhance trust in the resolution process. Additionally, providing avenues for appeal or review can ensure that decisions are fair and just. Maintaining high ethical standards and accountability is crucial for upholding the integrity of dispute resolution mechanisms.

Managing Costs and Resources

Managing costs and resources is a critical consideration in improving dispute resolution mechanisms. High legal and administrative costs can be a barrier for smaller shipping companies and shippers, limiting their access to justice. Streamlining procedures and reducing unnecessary costs can make dispute resolution more accessible. Additionally, providing financial assistance or subsidies for smaller parties can help level the playing field. Efficient resource management is essential for ensuring that dispute resolution mechanisms are sustainable and effective.

Promoting Early Resolution

Promoting early resolution of disputes can prevent escalation and reduce the overall burden on dispute resolution mechanisms. Encouraging parties to address conflicts promptly and proactively can minimize the impact on their operations and relationships. This can involve providing resources and incentives for early settlement, such as pre-dispute mediation services or expedited arbitration procedures. Early resolution not only saves time and costs but also preserves commercial relationships and fosters a collaborative industry environment.

Integrating Environmental Considerations

Integrating environmental considerations into dispute resolution mechanisms is increasingly important for the maritime industry. Disputes involving environmental damage or regulatory compliance require specialized knowledge and expertise. Developing guidelines and training for handling environmental disputes can ensure that these issues are addressed effectively. Additionally, promoting environmentally responsible practices within the industry can prevent disputes related to environmental impact. Balancing commercial interests with environmental protection is crucial for sustainable maritime trade.

Developing Standardized Procedures

Developing standardized procedures for dispute resolution can enhance consistency and predictability. Standardized procedures provide clear guidelines for parties and practitioners, reducing uncertainty and the potential for disputes. This can involve creating model arbitration and mediation clauses, standardized forms and templates, and procedural rules. Standardization can also facilitate training and education, ensuring that practitioners are familiar with best practices. Consistent procedures contribute to a more reliable and efficient dispute resolution system.

Enhancing Training and Education

Enhancing training and education for practitioners and parties involved in maritime disputes is essential for improving dispute resolution mechanisms. Comprehensive training programs can provide the necessary knowledge and skills for effectively handling disputes. This includes training on legal principles, procedural rules, negotiation techniques, and cultural sensitivity. Providing ongoing education and professional development opportunities ensures that practitioners stay updated on the latest developments and best practices. Well-trained professionals contribute to more effective and fair dispute resolution.

Utilizing Data and Analytics

Utilizing data and analytics can improve the efficiency and effectiveness of dispute resolution mechanisms. Analyzing data on dispute resolution outcomes, trends, and performance can provide valuable insights for enhancing procedures and policies. Data-driven decision-making can identify areas for improvement and optimize resource allocation. Additionally, predictive analytics can help anticipate and prevent disputes by identifying potential risks and issues early. Leveraging technology and data can drive continuous improvement in dispute resolution mechanisms.

Incorporating Feedback and Continuous Improvement

Incorporating feedback from parties and practitioners involved in dispute resolution can drive continuous improvement. Regularly soliciting feedback on procedures, outcomes, and experiences can identify strengths and areas for improvement. Creating mechanisms for feedback, such as surveys, focus groups, and review panels, ensures that the perspectives of stakeholders are considered. Continuous improvement efforts should focus on enhancing efficiency, fairness, and accessibility. Engaging stakeholders in the improvement process fosters a collaborative and responsive dispute resolution system.

Ensuring Global Relevance

Ensuring the global relevance of dispute resolution mechanisms is crucial for addressing the diverse needs of the maritime industry. The global nature of maritime trade requires mechanisms that are adaptable to different legal, cultural, and commercial contexts. This involves developing flexible procedures that can be tailored to specific circumstances and jurisdictions. Promoting international cooperation and harmonization can enhance the global applicability of dispute resolution mechanisms. Ensuring that these mechanisms are relevant and effective on a global scale is essential for supporting international maritime trade.

Future Prospects and Innovations

Looking ahead, the future of dispute resolution in the maritime industry holds promising prospects for innovation and improvement. Embracing new technologies, such as artificial intelligence and smart contracts, can further enhance efficiency and accuracy. AI-powered tools can assist in analyzing legal documents, predicting outcomes, and facilitating negotiations. Smart contracts can automate and streamline dispute resolution processes. Additionally, fostering a culture of collaboration and continuous learning within the maritime industry can drive ongoing advancements. By embracing innovation and adapting to changing needs, the maritime industry can develop dispute resolution mechanisms that are efficient, fair, and resilient.

Conclusion

In conclusion, improving dispute resolution mechanisms in the maritime industry is essential for addressing the complexities and challenges of global trade. By enhancing arbitration and mediation processes, establishing specialized maritime courts, and incorporating technological advancements, the industry can develop more efficient, accessible, and fair resolution systems. Balancing formal and informal methods, promoting international cooperation, and ensuring transparency and accountability are crucial for building trust and confidence. Addressing environmental considerations, managing costs, and promoting early resolution further contribute to effective dispute resolution. Continuous improvement efforts, driven by data, feedback, and innovation, can ensure that dispute resolution mechanisms remain relevant and effective in a rapidly evolving maritime landscape.

Encyclopedia   - **THE PATRON** -   .451

TOPIC 13:

Comprehensive Analysis: ON

Practical Scenarios in Carriage of Goods by Sea

Marwan M. Alarjan   - **MASTR** -   Martin Apollo Bureau

1. Scenario: Goods Damaged During Transit

Consider a scenario where a shipment of electronics is transported from China to the United States under a CIF (Cost, Insurance, and Freight) contract. Upon arrival, the buyer discovers that a significant portion of the goods is damaged due to rough sea conditions. In this situation, the CIF contract ensures that the seller has already arranged for insurance, so the buyer can file a claim with the insurance company to recover the losses. The buyer must provide evidence of the damage, such as survey reports and photos, to support the insurance claim. This scenario highlights the importance of comprehensive insurance coverage in protecting the buyer's interests during sea transit.

2. Scenario: Late Delivery and Penalties

In another scenario, a European car manufacturer orders a shipment of steel from Brazil, with the delivery deadline critical to maintaining production schedules. The shipment is delayed due to port congestion at the departure port, causing a halt in production and substantial financial losses for the manufacturer. Under the terms of a CIF contract, the risk and costs after shipment are on the buyer. However, if the delay was within the seller's control before the goods were loaded onto the vessel, the seller might be liable for breach of contract. The manufacturer can claim damages for the delay, emphasizing the need for clear contract terms regarding delivery deadlines and penalties.

3. Scenario: Misdelivery of Goods

Imagine a scenario where a shipment of raw materials is sent from India to Japan, but upon arrival, the goods are delivered to the wrong consignee due to an error in the bill of lading. The rightful consignee, upon not receiving the goods, would need to resolve the issue through legal means, potentially involving the carrier's liability for misdelivery. This situation underscores the critical role of the bill of lading as a document of title and the need for accurate and precise documentation in maritime trade.

4. Scenario: Dispute Over Freight Charges

A small business in Australia imports furniture from Indonesia under a C&F (Cost and Freight) contract, which covers the cost of transport to the destination port but excludes insurance. Upon receiving an invoice from the carrier, the business disputes additional freight charges that were not specified in the initial agreement. This dispute may need to be resolved through mediation or arbitration, where the terms of the contract and the applicable international conventions, such as the Hague-Visby Rules, would be examined to determine the legitimacy of the charges. This scenario highlights the importance of clear contractual agreements and understanding the scope of freight charges.

5. Scenario: Piracy and Risk Allocation

Consider a high-risk route where a shipment of pharmaceuticals from South Africa to the Middle East passes through waters known for piracy. Under an FOB (Free on Board) contract, the buyer assumes all risks once the goods pass the ship's rail. If the ship is hijacked and the goods are stolen, the buyer bears the loss unless additional marine insurance specifically covering piracy was arranged. This scenario emphasizes the necessity for both parties to assess and mitigate risks through appropriate insurance and risk management strategies.

6. Scenario: Environmental Compliance and Fines

A shipping company operating under an FAS (Free Alongside Ship) contract transports chemicals from Russia to Germany. Upon inspection at the destination port, authorities find that the ship did not comply with the latest environmental regulations regarding the discharge of ballast water. The company faces hefty fines and possible sanctions. The responsibility for compliance with environmental regulations lies with the carrier, and this incident stresses the importance of staying informed and compliant with international environmental standards to avoid legal and financial repercussions.

7. Scenario: Customs Delays and Perishable Goods

A shipment of fresh fruits is sent from Spain to Saudi Arabia under a CIF contract. Upon arrival, the shipment is held up at customs due to incomplete documentation. Given the perishable nature of the goods, any delay can result in significant losses. In this case, the buyer might claim damages for the loss of goods, while the seller could be liable for not ensuring proper documentation. This scenario illustrates the importance of meticulous paperwork and coordination with customs authorities to avoid delays and losses in the shipment of perishable goods.

8. Scenario: Shortage of Delivered Goods

An American retailer orders textiles from Bangladesh, and the goods are shipped under a CIF contract. When the shipment arrives, the retailer finds a shortage in the number of items received. The retailer can claim against the insurance for the shortfall, but must first determine whether the shortage occurred during transit or before the goods were loaded. A thorough inspection and documentation process is necessary to support the claim. This scenario highlights the necessity for robust inspection and documentation protocols both before and after shipment.

9. Scenario: Contract Termination and Goods in Transit

A European electronics manufacturer cancels an order for components from a Chinese supplier after the goods have already been shipped under a C&F contract. The goods are still in transit, and the buyer refuses to accept them at the destination port. The carrier, in this case, faces a dilemma regarding the storage or return of the goods and potential claims for unpaid freight charges. This situation underscores the complexity of handling contract terminations and the importance of clear terms regarding such eventualities in the contract.

10. Scenario: Technological Disruptions

In a modern scenario, a ship carrying high-tech equipment from South Korea to the United States encounters a cyber-attack that disrupts its navigation systems, causing a delay in delivery. The goods are insured under a CIF contract, but the buyer and seller must determine liability for the delay caused by the cyber-attack. This scenario highlights emerging risks in maritime trade due to technological advancements and the need for updated insurance policies and risk management strategies to address such issues.

These practical scenarios in the carriage of goods by sea illustrate the diverse challenges and complexities involved in maritime trade. They emphasize the importance of clear contractual terms, comprehensive insurance coverage, meticulous documentation, compliance with regulations, and proactive risk management strategies to ensure the smooth execution of international sales transactions.

TOPIC 14:

Advanced Logic Recommendations for Carriage by Sea

1. Risk Assessment and Management

- **Identify Risks**: Conduct thorough risk assessments for each shipment, considering factors such as the nature of the goods, routes, and potential hazards. Use advanced analytics and historical data to identify and quantify risks.

- **Mitigate Risks**: Implement risk mitigation strategies, such as diversifying shipping routes, using real-time tracking systems, and adopting advanced security measures to protect against theft and piracy. Invest in technologies like blockchain for secure documentation and tracking.

- **Insurance Coverage**: Ensure comprehensive insurance coverage that includes specific risks associated with maritime transport, such as piracy, cyber-attacks, and environmental hazards. Regularly review and update insurance policies to address emerging risks.

2. Optimization of Contract Terms

- **Tailored Contracts**: Customize contract terms based on the specific needs of each transaction. Use CIF contracts for shipments where the buyer prefers a single point of responsibility and FOB contracts when the buyer has strong logistical capabilities.

- **Clear Definitions**: Clearly define key terms, such as the point of risk transfer, delivery deadlines, and penalties for non-compliance. Ensure all parties understand their responsibilities and the implications of each contract type.

- **Incorporate Flexibility**: Include clauses that allow for adjustments in case of unforeseen events, such as natural disasters or geopolitical tensions. This can help prevent disputes and ensure continuity of trade.

3. Leveraging Technology

- **Digital Platforms**: Utilize digital platforms for booking, tracking, and managing shipments. Platforms that integrate blockchain technology can enhance transparency, reduce fraud, and streamline documentation processes.

- **Predictive Analytics**: Use predictive analytics to anticipate potential disruptions, optimize shipping routes, and improve supply chain efficiency. Advanced data analytics can help identify trends and make informed decisions.

- **Automated Systems**: Implement automated systems for monitoring and maintaining the condition of goods during transit, such as IoT devices for temperature-sensitive shipments. Automation can also assist in faster processing and clearance at ports.

4. Enhancing Legal and Regulatory Compliance

- **Stay Updated**: Regularly update knowledge on international maritime laws and conventions, such as the Hague-Visby Rules, Hamburg Rules, and Rotterdam Rules. Ensure compliance with environmental regulations and labor standards.

- **Customs and Documentation**: Ensure all customs documentation is accurate and complete to avoid delays. Use electronic documentation to expedite processes and reduce the risk of errors.

- **Training and Education**: Provide regular training for staff on the latest legal and regulatory requirements, best practices in shipping, and risk management strategies. This can help ensure compliance and reduce the likelihood of legal disputes.

5. Strengthening Dispute Resolution Mechanisms

- **Arbitration and Mediation**: Include arbitration and mediation clauses in contracts to provide efficient and less adversarial means of resolving disputes. Select reputable arbitration institutions and ensure clarity in the terms of arbitration.

- **Specialized Maritime Courts**: Advocate for the establishment or utilization of specialized maritime courts for resolving complex disputes that require specific expertise in maritime law.

- **Proactive Dispute Management**: Develop a proactive approach to dispute management by maintaining open communication channels between all parties and addressing potential issues before they escalate.

6. Sustainable and Green Shipping Practices

- **Environmental Compliance**: Ensure strict adherence to environmental regulations, such as MARPOL (Marine Pollution) and IMO (International Maritime Organization) guidelines. Invest in eco-friendly technologies and practices to reduce the environmental impact of shipping.

- **Carbon Footprint Reduction**: Implement measures to reduce the carbon footprint of shipping operations, such as using cleaner fuels, optimizing routes for fuel efficiency, and retrofitting ships with energy-efficient technologies.

- **Sustainability Reporting**: Maintain transparency in environmental practices by regularly reporting on sustainability metrics and initiatives. Engage in industry-wide efforts to promote sustainability and share best practices.

7. Collaboration and Partnerships

- **Strategic Alliances**: Form strategic alliances with other stakeholders in the supply chain, including shipping companies, port authorities, and logistics providers. Collaboration can enhance efficiency, reduce costs, and improve risk management.

- **Public-Private Partnerships**: Engage in public-private partnerships to leverage government support for infrastructure improvements, security enhancements, and regulatory compliance.

- **Industry Forums**: Participate in industry forums and trade associations to stay informed about the latest trends, regulations, and technological advancements. Networking can provide valuable insights and foster collaboration.

Conclusion

By integrating these advanced logic recommendations, businesses involved in the carriage of goods by sea can enhance efficiency, reduce risks, and ensure compliance with legal and regulatory requirements. These strategies will help navigate the complexities of maritime trade and contribute to sustainable and profitable operations.

TOPIC 15:

Upcoming Question:

The **"M/V Ever Given" incident** in March 2021 is often considered one of the biggest cases in the carriage by the sea law due to its far-reaching implications for global trade, legal complexities, and the staggering financial and logistical impacts it caused.

Overview of the M/V Ever Given Incident

On March 23, 2021, the Ever Given, a 400-meter-long container ship operated by Evergreen Marine, ran aground in the Suez Canal, blocking one of the world's most vital maritime trade routes for six days. The blockage halted nearly 12% of global trade, disrupting supply chains and costing billions of dollars in delayed goods.

Legal and Financial Implications

1. **Carrier Liability**:

    ◦ The Ever Given incident raised significant questions regarding the liability of the ship's owner and operator for the massive financial losses incurred due to the blockage.

    ◦ The legal framework governing such incidents typically involves principles of maritime law, including the shipowner's duty to ensure safe navigation and the responsibilities of the vessel's master and crew.

2. **General Average**:

- ○ The principle of General Average was invoked, a maritime law concept where all parties involved in a sea venture proportionately share the losses resulting from a sacrifice of part of the ship or cargo to save the whole in an emergency.
- ○ This principle led to complex calculations and contributions from various cargo owners whose goods were onboard the vessel.

3. **Insurance Claims**:

    ◦ The incident triggered a multitude of insurance claims, including those related to hull insurance, cargo insurance, and business interruption insurance.
    ◦ Determining the extent of coverage and liabilities involved numerous stakeholders, including shipowners, charterers, cargo owners, and insurers.

Case Complexity

1. **Multijurisdictional Issues:**

    ◦ The Ever Given incident involved multiple jurisdictions, including Egypt (where the canal is located), Panama (the flag state of the vessel), Japan (home to the shipowner), and various countries representing the cargo owners.

    ◦ Coordinating legal proceedings across these jurisdictions added to the complexity of resolving the incident.

2. **Salvage Operations:**

    ○   The technical and legal aspects of the salvage operations were significant. The efforts to free the ship required coordination between the Suez Canal Authority, international salvage companies, and other maritime experts.
    ○   Salvage claims and compensation for the salvage operations also formed a crucial part of the legal proceedings.

3. **Impact on Global Supply Chains:**

    ◦ The blockage's ripple effects on global supply chains were profound, affecting industries worldwide and highlighting the vulnerability of maritime chokepoints.

    ◦ Legal disputes arose from delayed shipments, contract breaches, and financial losses across various sectors.

Case Outcomes and Precedents

1. **Settlement and Compensation:**

    ○ After intense negotiations, the Suez Canal Authority (SCA) and the ship's insurers reached a settlement agreement. The ship was released from detention after an undisclosed compensation was agreed upon.

    ○ This settlement avoided prolonged legal battles but left many legal questions about liability and compensation unresolved in public discourse.

2. **Regulatory and Policy Changes:**

    ○   The incident prompted calls for reviewing and strengthening regulations governing the navigation and safety of large vessels in critical waterways.

    ○   Discussions on enhancing the legal frameworks for salvage operations, insurance coverage, and general average contributions have been part of the ongoing industry debate.

3. **Future Legal Implications:**

    ○ The Ever Given case is likely to influence future legal interpretations and policies regarding carrier liability, the application of general average, and the handling of similar maritime incidents.

    ○ It also serves as a precedent for the financial and legal preparedness required for managing large-scale maritime disruptions.

Advanced Question for Analysis :

Given the complexities and far-reaching impacts of the Ever Given incident, what lessons can be drawn about the adequacy of current international maritime laws and regulations in addressing such large-scale disruptions ?

How should legal frameworks evolve to better manage the risks and liabilities associated with global maritime trade, and what role should international cooperation play in this evolution ?

— Conclusion —

The carriage of goods by sea is a cornerstone of international trade, governed by a complex and evolving body of maritime law. International conventions such as the Hague-Visby Rules, Hamburg Rules, and Rotterdam Rules provide the legal framework for regulating the rights and responsibilities of carriers and shippers. Bills of lading, as fundamental documents in maritime trade, have significant legal implications for the parties involved. These legal instruments and conventions collectively ensure the smooth and predictable conduct of maritime commerce, facilitating the efficient movement of goods across the globe.

Carriers and shippers face various liabilities, and recent developments, such as the Ever Given and MSC Zoe incidents, highlight the challenges and legal complexities in maritime law. The Ever Given incident in the Suez Canal underscored the potential for massive economic disruptions and the intricate web of legal responsibilities and liabilities that arise in maritime trade. Similarly, the MSC Zoe incident, which involved the loss of containers in rough seas, brought to light the environmental and legal repercussions of such events. These cases demonstrate the importance of robust legal frameworks and effective risk management strategies in addressing the multifaceted challenges of maritime operations.

Regulatory fragmentation, complexity, and environmental concerns are ongoing challenges that need to be addressed through harmonization, digitalization, and sustainable practices. The disparate adoption of international conventions and varying national regulations contribute to legal uncertainties and inefficiencies. Harmonizing these regulations is crucial for creating a cohesive legal environment that supports international trade. Additionally, the integration of digital technologies can streamline maritime operations, enhance transparency, and reduce administrative burdens. Adopting sustainable practices is essential for mitigating the environmental impact of shipping and ensuring the industry's long-term viability.

Potential reforms and evolving trends, such as improved liability frameworks, enhanced dispute resolution mechanisms, and the adoption of green shipping technologies, will shape the future of maritime law. Revisiting liability limits and frameworks to reflect modern trade practices and risks can provide clearer guidelines for parties involved in maritime trade. Enhanced dispute resolution mechanisms, including greater use of arbitration and mediation, can offer more efficient and accessible means of resolving conflicts. The adoption of green shipping technologies, driven by regulatory requirements and industry initiatives, will play a critical role in reducing the environmental footprint of maritime operations.

By addressing these challenges and embracing these trends, the maritime industry can continue to facilitate global trade while adapting to the changing legal, technological, and environmental landscape. The dynamic nature of maritime law necessitates continuous evolution and proactive reforms to meet the demands of modern maritime commerce. Stakeholders, including international organizations, national governments, and industry players, must collaborate to develop and implement effective legal and regulatory frameworks. This collaborative approach will ensure that maritime law remains responsive to emerging challenges, promoting a sustainable and efficient global shipping industry.

PART TWO END

PREVIOUS PARTS

1. PART I : INTERNATIONAL TRAD LAW

UPCOMING PARTS

1. PART III : INTELLECTUAL PROPERTY RIGHTS AND COMPETITION LAW & ELECTRONIC COMMERCE AND DIGITAL TRADE

2. PART IV : CROSS-BORDER MERGERS AND ACQUISITIONS & INTERNATIONAL CORPORATE LAW AND GOVERNANCE

3. PART V : INTERNATIONAL ARBITRATION AND DISPUTE RESOLUTION & INTERNATIONAL INVESTMENT LAW

4. PART VI : INTERNATIONAL FINANCIAL REGULATION & INTERNATIONAL TRADE FINANCE

5. PART VII : INTERNATIONAL TAXATION AND TRANSFER PRICING & ENVIRONMENTAL AND SOCIAL ASPECTS OF INTERNATIONAL TRADE LAW

6. PART VIII : ADVANCED CONTRACT LAW AND NEGOTIATION & ADVANCED RESEARCH METHODS OF LAW

CONTINUES ..

www.ingramcontent.com/pod-product-compliance
Lightning Source LLC
Chambersburg PA
CBHW020623220526
45464CB00001B/6